COMMUNITY UNIT SCH. DIST. #11
JR. H. S. LIBRARY
HOOPESTON, ILLINOIS

WWII

HIROSHIMA & NAGASAKI

WORLD

TURNING POINTS OF WAR II
HIROSHIMA AND NAGASAKI

COMMUNITY UNIT SCH. DIST. #11
AR. H. S. LIBRARY
HOOPESTON, ILLINOIS

Chapter 2

JANE CLAYPOOL

FRANKLIN WATTS ▪ 1984
NEW YORK ▪ LONDON ▪ TORONTO ▪ SYDNEY

Picture research by Roberta Guerette, Omni Photo Communication

MANY THANKS TO THE STAFF OF THE
BERKSHIRE ATHENEUM, PITTSFIELD, MASSACHUSETTS

Photographs courtesy of: Culver Pictures Inc.: pp. 5, 46;
UPI: pp. 7, 12, 13, 34, 35, 57, 68, 71, 75, 80, 90, 91, 96, 97.

Maps by Vantage Art, Inc.

Library of Congress Cataloging in Publication Data

Miner, Claypool, Jane
Hiroshima and Nagasaki.

(Turning points of World War II)
Includes bibliographical references and index.
Summary: Discusses the planning for and the aftermath
of the American use of the atomic bomb which destroyed
two Japanese cities in August 1945.
1. Hiroshima-shi (Japan)—Bombardment, 1945—Juvenile
literature. 2. Nagasaki-shi (Japan)—Bombardment, 1945—
Juvenile literature. 3. Atomic bomb—History—Juvenile
literature. 4. World War, 1939-1945—Japan—Juvenile literature
5. Japan—History—1912-1945—Juvenile literature. [1. Hiroshima-shi
(Japan)—Bombardment, 1945. 2. Nagasaki-shi (Japan)—Bombardment,
1945. 3. Atomic bomb—History. 4. World War, 1939-1945—Japan.
5. Japan—History—1912-1945] I. Title. II. Series.
D767.25.H6M46 1984   940.54′26   84-7325
ISBN 0-531-04862-4

Copyright © 1984 by Jane Claypool
All rights reserved
Printed in the United States of America
6 5

CONTENTS

CHAPTER ONE
Hiroshima 1

CHAPTER TWO
The Early Work 19

CHAPTER THREE
The Race Is On 27

CHAPTER FOUR
The Manhattan Project 39

CHAPTER FIVE
Truman Becomes President in a Troubled World 51

CHAPTER SIX
Trinity 61

CHAPTER SEVEN
The Decision to Use the Bomb 73

CHAPTER EIGHT
The Aftermath 93

For Further Reading 101

Index 103

IN MEMORY OF
ROBERT BRUCE WHITAKER

HIROSHIMA

In August 1945 World War II was drawing to a slow, bloody conclusion. The United States and her Allies, Great Britain and Russia, had already defeated Germany and reclaimed France and other European countries from Hitler's Nazi Germany. In Europe the battle was over and the peacetime problems of rebuilding and reconstruction had begun. Meanwhile, the war against the Japanese in the South Pacific dragged on.

No one doubted that the Japanese would eventually have to surrender; they were outnumbered, and they were running out of economic resources. Now that the Nazis were defeated, the total attention of the United States and Great Britain would be devoted to defeating the Japanese. However, no one was sure when victory in the Pacific would come. Most military officials in the United States expected to have to invade Japan and fight from house to house. Almost four years in the South Pacific, fighting for atolls and islands, had convinced United States military leaders that the Japanese were determined, powerful fighters. The United States military and political leaders dreaded a bloody invasion of the Japanese mainland, but few believed it could be avoided.

On August 6, 1945, the United States dropped an atomic bomb on Hiroshima, Japan. Three days later, it dropped a second one on another Japanese city, Nagasaki. Those two bombs were the first and only atomic weapons ever used in actual combat. Until the news was reported in *The New York Times* on August 7, 1945, most American citizens had never even heard of atomic bombs. Only a handful of leaders and scientists knew they were being developed.

While atomic bombs were different and more terrible, people had grown accustomed to reading about tremendous bombing damage. Ordinary bombs had been an important part of World War II, and they brought much destruction to both sides. The Germans had haunted European skies from 1939 until 1942 as their *Luftwaffe* bombers tried to weaken Great Britain enough to make invasion possible. Night after night, they bombarded the British islands. As the English fought back, the losses of life and property were devastating. Over twenty-five hundred German and British planes were lost in the Battle of Britain in 1940.

On each side, bombers blasted the enemy's lands. Just as the Germans had bombed targets in Britain, American and British planes smashed railroad lines and destroyed factories and cities in Germany. Throughout the war casualties were high and the damage that bombers did to civilians as well as military targets was devastating. For instance, Allied bombers raided the German town of Hamburg several times between July 24 and August 3, 1943. They killed an estimated forty-three thousand people, most of them civilians.

Heavy bombing and many casualties were common during the war. While people were horrified, few protested the need since both sides were using sophisticated aircraft and deadly bombs. The United States' B-29s were sophisticated and powerful bombers that probably did a great deal to win the war against Germany. The German V-2 rockets were devastating weapons that did tremendous damage to Great Britain. Only the United States escaped being bombed on its mainland; however, many men were killed by bombs in North Africa, the South Pacific, and other places where American troops fought.

For a great part, World War II was a battle of weapons.

The country that could design and produce the most effective weapons would win. More than any other country, the United States understood the importance of technological warfare, and its tremendous effort to produce ships, airplanes, and other weapons resulted in fewer casualties on the battlefield in proportion to other fighting nations.

In the light of these facts it is not difficult to understand why the United States worked so hard to build atomic weapons once their use became theoretically feasible. They were bombs, but these bombs were bigger and more effective than anything anyone could have imagined in an earlier war. Even after they were used, most people found it difficult to imagine their power and the damage they could do.

Today, many people question the wisdom of having used the atomic bombs against Japan. In 1945, during the desperate struggle to end the war and bring our servicemen home, the news of the atomic bombs was greeted with rejoicing. Few people understood the principles behind the weapons, but they did understand that the bomb would keep American soldiers from the dreaded mainland invasion. Faced with the total destruction caused by atomic weapons, even the proud and determined Japanese military men would have to capitulate.

Though the reporting after the bombs were dropped was as honest as it could be, the whole development project had been shrouded in absolute secrecy. Because of this, and because few people could imagine the amount of destruction that the atomic bombs brought, it was months and years before the American people understood the full impact of those bombs on the Japanese people and on the world.

Even the crew that dropped the bomb on Hiroshima was unprepared for the extent of the damage. Two days before the flight, crew members were shown films of the only atomic-bomb test ever made at Alamogordo, New Mexico. At that time, Navy Captain William S. Parsons, who was in charge of assembling the bomb, told the crew that no one could be sure what would happen when it was dropped over

Colonel Paul Tibbets gives last-minute instructions to the crew of the Enola Gay *before they take off for Hiroshima.*

a Japanese city. The crew knew they were flying a special weapon from the Pacific island of Tinian to the city of Hiroshima, but no one used the words atomic bomb.

Despite the uncertainty and lack of experience surrounding the mission, everything went very well. There were seven B-29s assigned to the mission—three as weather planes, one as a stand-by, two to carry scientific equipment and observers, and the *Enola Gay* to carry the bomb. The *Enola Gay* was named by the pilot, Colonel Paul Tibbets, after his mother. The atomic bomb also had a name, "Little Boy."

The weight of the bomb and the 7,600 gallons of fuel the *Enola Gay* carried made takeoff very difficult. In fact, no one was sure whether the plane would actually be able to lift off the ground. For this reason, it was decided to finish the final assembly of the bomb in the air. That way, if there was an accident, the crew of the plane would certainly be lost, but the men and equipment on the island of Tinian would probably be safe.

The *Enola Gay* took off on schedule, the weather was good, the bombing was right on time and no casualties were suffered by the United States. Copilot Robert Lewis later remembered, "The bomb run was just as uneventful as the trip up there and everything went just about the way it was programmed to go."

The bomb was dropped from an altitude of 31,600 feet (9,632 m); forty-three seconds later, it detonated at 1,800 feet (549 m) over Hiroshima. Navigator Theodore Van Kirk reported,

> There was a bright flash . . . like a photographer's flashbulb exploding in the plane. . . . The plane bounced, it jumped and there was a noise like a piece of sheet metal snapping. Those of us who had flown quite a bit over Europe thought that it was antiaircraft fire that had exploded very close to the plane.

Hiroshima, August 6, 1945.

But there was no antiaircraft fire. In fact, there was no resistance of any sort, so complete was the devastation below. Colonel Paul Tibbets brought the *Enola Gay* back to a course that allowed the crew to take a look at Hiroshima lying below them.

Copilot Lewis recalled:

> I don't believe anyone ever expected to look at a sight quite like that. Where we had seen a clear city two minutes before, we could now no longer see the city. We could see smoke and fires creeping up the sides of the mountain . . .

Navigator Van Kirk described it this way, "If you want to describe it as something you are familiar with, a pot of boiling black oil . . . "

Another crew member asked aloud, "My God, what have we done?"

But the crew's descriptions were not equal to the devastation they were seeing. Hiroshima had been almost obliterated. The bomb exploded 1,800 feet (549 m) above the center of the city and 60 percent of the city's area—more than 4 square miles (10 sq km)—was absolutely erased. Beyond that utter destruction, houses were knocked flat as far as 3 miles (4.8 km) from the center zone of devastation. Eighty percent of all the buildings in Hiroshima were destroyed, and the rest were badly damaged.

No one knows exactly how many people were killed in the initial blast, because thousands disappeared without a trace. The official estimates vary between seventy thousand and eighty thousand, with as many injured. Of course, no one predicted the horrible, lingering deaths of the thousands who would die from radiation effects days, months, and years later.

The citizens of Hiroshima who survived the blast have testified that the effect of the bomb was unimaginable. Some actually saw the bomb, followed by its parachute, falling from the sky. Then there was a tremendous fireball of white light. The fireball was a hundred times brighter than the sun, at least 250 feet (76 m) in diameter. The fireball was the same temperature as the sun.

The explosion was indescribably loud, and it was accompanied by a wave of concussion that flattened 6,820 buildings and badly damaged 3,750 more. Then the fireball sucked up millions of tons of dust and debris and formed a mushroom cloud that rained radioactive material on the city. Of the approximately 300,000 inhabitants of Hiroshima, more than a fourth were instantly incapacitated or dead. All means of communication were gone. Eighty percent of the firefighting personnel could not respond to the alarms; most were killed or wounded. Seventy percent of the firefighting equipment was destroyed. Water mains broke and pipes melted in the heat. Of the city's forty-five hospitals, only three were standing. Only twenty-eight of the 290 physicians in the city were unhurt; only 126 of the 1,780 nurses. The city was a blaze of fire, and it burned for three days.

Accounts from the survivors of the Hiroshima blast are shocking tales of suffering. One such account may illustrate some of the horror encountered. Tsutomu Yanaguchi, a shipbuilder, was badly burned by the blast. He ran from his factory into a field, where five teenage boys ran toward him. They were naked and covered with blood. He says,

> As the boys came near, I saw they were pale, and shaking severely. . . . I have never seen such a horrifying sight as those five shivering boys. Blood was pouring in streams from deep cuts all over their bodies, mingling with their perspiration, and their skin was burned deep red, like the color of cooked lobsters. At first it seemed, strangely, that their burned and lacerated backs and chests were growing green grass! Then I saw that hundreds of blades of sharp grass had been driven deep into their flesh, evidently by the force of the blast.

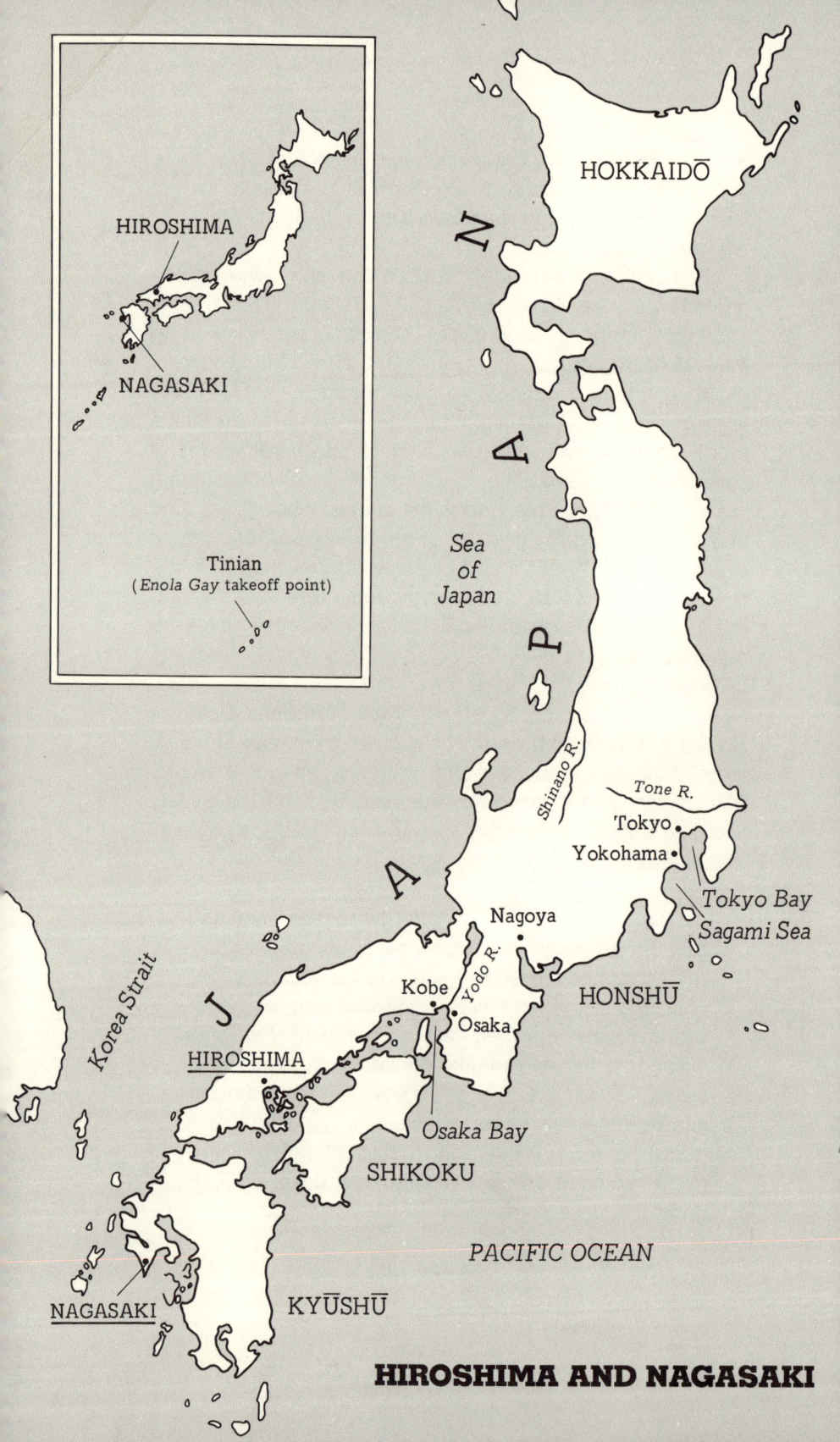

None of the Americans involved in the planning could have predicted the extent of destruction in Hiroshima, though they knew it would be tremendously powerful. Three months before, Dr. J. Robert Oppenheimer, chief scientist for the atomic-bomb project, had testified before the president's Interim Committee. At that time, he estimated that no more than twenty thousand Japanese would be killed in the attack. What did not occur to him, or anyone else, was that two lone B-29s would fail to frighten the citizens of Hiroshima enough to force them into their air-raid shelters.

Until that day, Hiroshima had been generally spared from bombing. While the five biggest industrial centers— Tokyo, Nagoya, Osaka, Kobe, and Yokahama—had been devastated by bombs, Hiroshima was almost untouched. What's more, the citizens were used to seeing one or two lone planes on photo reconnaissance missions. The photo planes did not drop bombs, so when the *Enola Gay* flew overhead on the morning of August 6, 1945, the workers and citizens of Hiroshima were going on with their routine lives. Had they gone to bomb shelters, many probably would have been saved.

For the citizens of Hiroshima, the bomb was a nightmare that would last for many years. Victims who did not die outright would suffer from radiation sickness, permanent maiming, and despair. The city of Hiroshima thrives today, but the memory of August 6, 1945 remains imprinted on the consciousness of the people of Hiroshima and the nation of Japan.

In the United States, the news of the atomic bomb was greeted with elation. The first news reports were printed in *The New York Times* on Tuesday, August 7, 1945. Until that time, the development of the atomic bomb had been a closely guarded secret. When the people of the United States learned of the bombing of Hiroshima, most were overjoyed. They were ready to do anything to end the fighting and bring the American soldiers home.

The Japanese had had no description or specific warning

Scenes of Hiroshima after the atomic bomb blast. Above: ash covers concrete structures that survived the explosion; Opposite: soldiers of the U.S. occupation force survey the desolate scene of a charred bus whose occupants were killed when the bomb fell.

of the devastating weapon, though the Potsdam Conference that had ended a few days earlier had resulted in a general threat. At Potsdam, the Allies had issued an ultimatum that called for an unconditional surrender. The ultimatum had apparently been ignored. In reporting the atomic bomb attack, *The New York Times* quoted President Truman as saying:

> It was to spare the Japanese people from utter destruction that the ultimatum of July 26 was issued at Potsdam. Their leaders promptly rejected that ultimatum. If they do not now accept our terms, they may expect a rain of ruin from the air the like of which has never been seen on this earth.

Three days after the bombing of Hiroshima, when the Japanese government did not respond with an immediate and unconditional surrender, a second bomb was dropped on Nagasaki. Called "Fat Man," it was a plutonium bomb. Though based on the same principles, the first and second bombs were constructed with different fuels, uranium and plutonium, and were ignited by two different methods. The bomb dropped on Hiroshima was based on splitting an atom of uranium (U-235) and was ignited by the gun-assembly method. The bomb dropped on Nagasaki and the one tested earlier at Alamogordo, New Mexico, were based on splitting an atom of plutonium and were ignited by the implosion method. While both bombs were devastating, the second one was more powerful.

New York Times science reporter, William L. Laurence, rode in an observation plane that accompanied the bomber, *Bock's Car*, that dropped the bomb on Nagasaki. These are the words Laurence used to describe the approach to that city:

> . . . at the very last minute, there came an opening (in the clouds). For a few brief moments Nagasaki stood out clearly in broad noontime daylight.

After the bomb was dropped, he described the blast,

> . . . a giant ball of fire rose as though from the bowels (and) a giant pillar of purple fire . . . shooting skyward with enormous speed.

He said of the mushroom cloud that it was,

> . . . even more alive . . . seething and boiling in a white fury of creamy foam, sizzling upward and then descending earthward, a thousand geysers rolled into one.

The second bomb was dropped on Nagasaki at 12:01 P.M. on August 9. The surprise of the people was great because the Japanese government had taken great pains to minimize knowledge of the extent of damage to Hiroshima. Calling it, "a special-type bomb," and not acknowledging the fact that it was an atomic weapon, the Japanese government had kept even top military leaders in the dark about the destruction of Hiroshima. While they debated the possibility of surrender, the Japanese parliament received the news that a second bomb had fallen on Nagasaki. This time, nearly a hundred thousand Japanese were killed or maimed in the bombing and the fires that followed. Twelve hours later fires in Nagasaki were burning so brightly that pilots two hundred miles away could see the blaze.

Japan accepted the Allied terms of surrender on August 14, 1945, eight days after the bomb was dropped on Hiroshima. In his announcement of intention to surrender, the Emperor of Japan included this statement:

> . . . I cannot endure the thought of letting my people suffer any longer. A continuation of the war would bring death to tens, perhaps even hundreds, of thousands of persons. The whole nation would be reduced to ashes.

There is little doubt that the use of the atomic bombs shortened World War II. When the news broke, American sentiment was overwhelmingly in favor of the decision to use the atomic bomb. Typical of the attitudes among servicemen was that of navigator Theodore Van Kirk, who flew on the *Enola Gay*. "I thought: Thank God the war is over and I don't have to get shot at anymore. I can go home."

President Truman justified his decision in exactly the same manner. After twenty years of silence about his private struggles with the decision to drop the atomic bomb, he told a television audience in February 1965:

> It was a question of saving hundreds of thousands of American lives. I don't mind telling you that you don't feel normal when you have to plan hundreds of complete, final deaths of American boys who are alive and joking and having fun while you are doing your planning. You break your heart and your head trying to figure out a way to save one life.
>
> The name given to our invasion plan was "Olympia," but I saw nothing godly about the killing of all the people that would be necessary to make an invasion of the Japanese mainland. The casualty estimates called for 750,000 Americans—250,000 killed, 500,000 maimed for life.
>
> I could not worry about what history would say about my personal morality. I made the only decision I ever knew how to make. I did what I thought was right.

Yet even at the time the bomb was dropped, there were doubts among the men who participated in the action. Dr. Luis Alvarez was an explosives specialist who rode with the *Enola Gay* on her mission. He felt compelled to write to his young son on the way back to base. The letter was a justification of his action and probably an attempt to forestall future criticism of the morning's events. He wrote, "Dear Walter,"

This is the first grown-up letter I have written to you, and it is really for you to read when you are older . . . What regrets I have about being a party to killing and maiming thousands of Japanese civilians this morning are tempered with the hope that this terrible weapon we have created may bring the countries of the world together and prevent further wars.

While the general feeling was jubilation that the war was over, it was not long before doubts began to set in. Criticism over the second bombing in Nagasaki was especially severe. Many objected that the Japanese government was too stunned by events in Hiroshima to react any quicker than they did. Three days was not long enough, critics argued, between the first and second bombs. Soon, the suspicion was voiced that the bomb on Nagasaki was deliberately dropped before the Japanese could surrender in order to test the effects of that more sophisticated plutonium bomb.

Others insisted that neither bombing was necessary to end the war. They suggested that the president might have invited the Japanese officials to a demonstration of the atomic test and warned them before they struck. Many of the physicists who had been involved in the development and testing of the atomic bomb later stated that they wished it had never been invented. Dr. J. Robert Oppenheimer, director of the Los Alamos laboratory Project that designed the atomic bomb, said publicly, "We have blood on our hands."

Debate about our use of the atomic bomb has raged for more than forty years. The questions remain, and as people examine the use of nuclear weapons in today's wars, the answers become even more difficult to obtain. Was the decision to use the atomic bomb morally correct? Was the development of the atomic bomb, as President Truman claimed, ". . . the greatest achievement of organized science in history"? Or was it, as J. Robert Oppenheimer later declared, ". . . a grievous error"?

CHAPTER II

THE EARLY WORK

COMMUNITY UNIT SCH. DIST. #11
JR. H. S. LIBRARY
HOOPESTON, ILLINOIS

The development of the atomic bomb was the best kept secret of World War II. When news of the attack on Hiroshima was published in the American newspapers, it surprised top military leaders, politicians, and scientists who were working on other war projects. It was so secret that some of the people working in the factories where the bomb was developed had no idea what they were working on.

The incredible secrecy surrounding the atomic project is even more surprising because right up until the eve of World War II, atomic research had been an internationally cooperative effort. Considered largely theoretical, atomic research information was exchanged freely among scientists of all nations until almost the beginning of World War II. As atomic research progressed and the possibility of building a bomb became less of a fantasy, European powers were faced with the possibility of war.

The international turmoil affected the lives of atomic scientists who were faced with choices about how they would use their special knowledge about atomic structure. If the theoretical possibility of splitting an atom and producing an immensely powerful weapon should become a practical possibility, then any scientific knowledge the individual scientist had was of tremendous importance to the political powers who would be involved in the war. Some scientists who were citizens of Germany changed their allegiance and devoted their special knowledge to the Allied cause. Most of these men and women were Jewish or had relatives who were Jewish. It is ironic that Hitler's anti-Semitic policies forced some of the finest scientific minds in his nation to choose the other side in the coming war. The defection of these Jewish scientists probably slowed German efforts to develop the atomic bomb and may have influenced the outcome of the war.

During World War II, atomic scientists were involved in a political and military struggle that forced them to work at fantastic speed to unravel the mystery of the atom. However, they were building on knowledge that had been discovered at a much more leisurely pace. In fact, atomic research began long before there were nations called Germany, Great Britain, or the United States of America.

In a sense, work on the atomic bomb began more than two thousand years ago with the Greek philosopher, Democritus. He was the first Westerner to develop the theory that matter is made up of small particles that cannot be divided into any smaller pieces. Our word atom comes from the Greek word, *atoma*, which means "that which cannot be cut."

For two thousand years, people talked about Democritus' theory but didn't really experiment with it. It was the famous scientist, Isaac Newton, who lived in England from 1642 until 1727, who revived the idea of atoms. He wrote:

> It seems probable to me that God in the beginning formed matter in solid . . . particles . . . even so very hard as never to wear or break into pieces; no ordinary power being able to divide what God himself made one in the first creation.

The discovery that atoms could be split came in stages of knowledge. The first stage was giving up the idea that the atom was the smallest piece of matter in the universe. Several scientists contributed to the description of the makeup of the atom. J.J. Thomson, a British physicist, first announced the discovery of the electron in 1897. He discovered that electrons, or small electrical particles inside the atom, are in constant motion and acting upon each other.

Ernest Rutherford, who was born in New Zealand and lived in Canada and Great Britain, enlarged on Thomson's work. He developed the theory of an atomic nucleus in 1911. Rutherford's work proved that the atom definitely was not solid, but spacious.

Though only thirty-six years would pass between Rutherford's laboratory experiments and the bombing of Hiroshima, none of the physicists working on atomic structure were thinking in practical terms of weaponry at that time. Their interest was purely scientific and their discoveries followed each other in rapid-fire succession.

Niels Bohr of Denmark was the scientist who first definitely identified the neutron. Bohr was awarded the Nobel Prize in 1922 for his work on the atom's structure. By that time, scientists were fairly clear about the structure of the atom.

An atom is so small that more than 250,000,000 hydrogen atoms would have to be lined up side by side to measure an inch. The hydrogen atom is the smallest in size but larger ones, such as uranium atoms, are only four times greater in diameter. Atoms are constantly in motion, moving at speeds of 1,300 feet (396 m) per second and faster. Inside every atom, electrons move around the nucleus in the same manner that our planets move around the sun. The nucleus that the electrons orbit contains two types of particles, the proton and the neutron. Protons are about two thousand times heavier than electrons and have a positive electrical charge. Neutrons are as heavy as protons but have no electrical charge.

Some atoms are more complex than others. For instance, a hydrogen atom is very simple because it contains only one proton in the nucleus and has one electron spinning about. The hydrogen atom is also the lightest weight atom. On the other hand, a uranium-238 atom has 92 protons and 146 neutrons in its nucleus and 92 electrons arranged in seven shells circling the nucleus.

Knowledge about the structure of the atom, combined with other scientific discoveries and theories, eventually produced the atom bomb. One important part of the scientific development was work done on radioactivity and X rays. In 1895 Wilhelm Conrad Roentgen of Germany discovered X rays. The next year, Henri Becquerel of France discovered natural radioactivity.

Following this line of scientific inquiry, Marie and Pierre Curie's research work on radioactivity led to the discovery of radium. Radium is naturally radioactive, meaning that certain of its atoms spontaneously disintegrate. The Curies' work would be the foundation for the eventual splitting of uranium atoms to produce a chain reaction. Uranium would be used as fuel for atomic bombs because of its complicated structure and natural radioactivity.

Albert Einstein's famous formula, $E = mc^2$, was another step toward the development of the atom bomb because the equation showed that mass and energy were aspects of the same thing. The energy (E) is the product of mass (m) and the velocity of light (c) squared (2). His work in 1905 earned him the title, "The Father of the Atom Bomb," though he never actually worked on an aspect of building the weapon.

What his early work made clear was that if a nucleus of an atom (mass) could be broken into two pieces of the same size, the total mass of those two pieces will be less than that of the original. The difference in the size of the mass is converted to energy. This process is called *fission*. The eventual construction of the atom bomb was based on the fission process, and Einstein understood the theoretical implications of his early work. He said that if the total nuclear energy in a pound of matter were to be released, it would be the same as exploding 10 million tons (9 million mt) of TNT. At that time there were so many barriers to making the theories practical that Einstein was sure that atomic energy was many lifetimes away.

Though his early work was only theoretical, Einstein was

one of the scientists to suffer from Hitler's anti-Semitic attacks. Einstein came to the United States in 1933, the year Adolf Hitler came to power. His work, along with that of Danish physicist Niels Bohr, had been criticized as "nothing but Jewish worldbluff" by Hitler. Einstein was one of the first Jews to lose his job and property.

Einstein was not the only scientist to suffer attacks from Hitler. One month after he came to power in 1933, Hitler threw seven famous Jewish physicists off the faculty of the world-famous University of Göttingen. German Jewish scientists began to leave Germany in 1933, and they continued to leave until the borders were closed by war. They searched for new homes where they could work in peace. Some, like Einstein, went directly to the United States. Others went to England to work at the Cavendish Laboratories at Cambridge University. Others, like Hungarian Edward Teller, went first to Denmark to work with Niels Bohr in Copenhagen. In the forties, nearly all the scientists who had gone to Denmark, and many who had gone to England, found their way to the United States.

In the twenties and thirties the three major centers of activity and knowledge in atomic research were in Europe: Bohr's research center in Copenhagen, Denmark, the Cavendish Laboratory in England, and the University of Göttingen in Germany. While these were the most important, scientists were working in many other centers and laboratories on atomic research, and they were reporting their findings openly. There was an international body of workers who contributed to the development of atomic fission. Men and women from many countries, including Greece, France, Austria, Hungary, Denmark, Germany, Japan, Czechoslovakia, Great Britain, and the United States worked on atomic experiments and discoveries. Even though scientists were having to leave their homelands and politicians were predicting war, scientific experiments were still considered to be the property of all scientists and atomic reseach was openly reported.

The experiment that triggered the closing of that open

exchange took place in 1938. Two German scientists, Otto Hahn and Fritz Strassmann split a uranium atom and reported their experiment to a former colleague, Lise Meitner. Because Hahn and Strassmann were chemists, not physicists, they were reluctant to draw conclusions about their experiment, so they simply reported the event.

Lise Meitner recognized that the Hahn-Strassmann experiment was actually atomic fission and reacted quickly to the news. She had worked on the same sort of experiments for years, often with Hahn and Strassmann, and she was excited by the apparent success of this latest work.

The process of atomic fission or atom splitting, is a procedure that includes shooting a neutron into the nucleus of an atom. If the neutron makes a direct hit, the neutrons inside the atom are freed and a great amount of energy is given off. Basically, this procedure is a tiny atomic explosion.

Once Meitner recognized that Hahn and Strassmann had actually produced atomic fission, she understood the implications and acted upon them. Splitting one atom was only of theoretical interest, but, if a way could be found to produce a chain reaction, it might mean a great deal to the nations that were squaring off for war. The Hahn-Strassmann experiment was proof that the possibility of using atomic fission to produce weapons was becoming a practical possibility instead of a theoretical idea.

Before an atomic bomb could be developed, a way would have to be found to set up a chain reaction in more complex elements such as uranium and plutonium, but that too was a possibility. A chain reaction would mean that the atom that was split would then split other atoms, producing a greater explosion.

No one knew how to produce a chain reaction but as a refugee from Nazi Germany, Meitner was very concerned that Germany not be the first country to use atomic power for weapons. She was living in Sweden at that time, but she had been a leading professor at the Kaiser Wilhelm Institute for Chemistry in Berlin since World War I. She had worked with

Hahn since 1907 and had received recognition for her atomic research, mostly on the physics of the atomic nucleus. Because she was Jewish, she had been forced to leave Germany, but she was close enough to Hahn and Strassmann to understand the experiments completely.

Meitner talked to her nephew, Otto Frisch, about her fears. He was also a refugee and working with Niels Bohr. Bohr agreed with Frisch and Meitner about the import of the Hahn-Strassmann experiment. On January 15, 1939, Otto Frisch reproduced the German experiment and proved conclusively that it was possible to crack a uranium nucleus and release energy. If a way could be found to produce a reliable chain reaction, it might be possible to build atomic weapons.

Since Hitler had already declared his intention to conquer the world and war seemed inevitable, some far-seeing scientists were certain that atomic research should be kept secret from Nazi Germany. But most of the people in the world had never heard of the possibility of atomic fission, and most scientists were dubious about the possibility of putting atomic research to any practical purpose.

The United States magazine, *Time,* ran a story about the Hahn-Strassmann experiment a few weeks later. The story spoke of the atom splitting as a "great accident" and went on to suggest possible peacetime uses of atomic fission some time in the far distant future. The last paragraph of the three-paragraph article said:

> Though the discovery does not raise an immediate prospect of driving ocean liners for thousands of miles with the atomic energy locked in a cupful of water, it does help justify the statement of popularizing physicists that such things would be possible if atomic energy could be efficiently released.

In 1939 atomic fission seemed to be a fantastic dream. Only five years later, it would be part of a real war that was a deadly nightmare.

THE RACE IS ON

Lise Meitner was not the only scientist-refugee from Nazi Germany to be alarmed at the possible uses Adolf Hitler might make of atomic research. The years 1938 and 1939 were years of tremendous upheaval and transition for many atomic scientists, many of whom left Germany just in time to escape death. Leo Szilard was a Hungarian refugee who went first to Denmark and later to the United States to work on the atomic bomb. In 1939 he began a campaign to persuade atomic scientists to keep all atomic research secret from Germany. He called for voluntary secrecy and asked that papers on atomic research not be published. Other scientists, including his fellow countryman, Edward Teller, agreed. By the time Hitler invaded Poland in September 1939, most atomic scientists were voluntarily silent about their work.

By then, many of the scientists who would develop the atomic bomb were settled in their new homes. Szilard and Teller were in the United States along with Italian physicist Enrico Fermi. Fermi, whose wife was Jewish, came to the United States in December 1938 because the Italian dictator, Benito Mussolini, had passed anti-Semitic laws and made such statements as, "Jews do not belong in the human race."

Fermi's work on atomic research was some of the most

advanced, and he immediately proposed to repeat an earlier atom-splitting experiment that he'd made as far back as 1934. After reading accounts of the Hahn-Strassmann work, he realized that he had actually performed a similar experiment five years earlier. He repeated the experiment at Columbia University in 1939, confirming the fact that he was actually the first scientist to split the atom, though he'd failed to identify it at the time.

Irene Joliot-Curie and her husband, Frederic Joliot-Curie, had also split the atom in experiments they performed in their laboratory in Paris in 1939. Like Enrico Fermi, they did not understand what they had done and did not label the experiment correctly.

The Joliot-Curies were awarded a Nobel Prize in 1935 for their work in carrying on the investigations of Marie and Pierre Curie. At that time, Frederic Joliot-Curie demonstrated his understanding of the possibilities of the work currently being done on atomic structure. He said, ". . . scientists who can construct and demolish elements at will may also be capable of causing nuclear transformations of an explosive character."

By the end of 1939 several scientists, including Frisch, Hahn, and Fermi, knew how to split the atom, or produce fission, by shooting a neutron into the nucleus of an atom of uranium. But the distance from that experiment to useful atomic power was a very long one. Splitting one atom released energy, but it was nothing more than a theoretical stunt. Unless it was possible to set up a nuclear chain reaction, the demonstration that the atom could be split would be of little use to anyone.

Each fission released about two hundred million electron volts of energy and threw off neutrons. Many scientists believed these neutrons could be used to set off a violent chain reaction if the technology could be perfected. Very simply, chain reaction can be compared to shooting a marble into a group of a hundred marbles. As the first marble hits, it sets other marbles into motion, which hit other marbles in turn. Thus, the group of marbles explode into action through chain reaction.

Since atomic fission of the uranium atom released at least two neutrons, then each of those two neutrons would split two more atoms which would release a total of four neutrons. Those four would split atoms, releasing at least eight neutrons. The explosion would continue so rapidly that in eighty steps, the number of atoms split would be a trillion trillion. (That's expressed by the number 1 followed by 24 zeros.) That is the approximate number of atoms found in a pound of uranium.

Leo Szilard, the Hungarian refugee and physicist who had been in Denmark with Bohr, was teaching at Columbia University in New York City when he demonstrated the possibility of building a chain reaction. Szilard and his colleague, Walter Zinn, set up a simple laboratory experiment to illustrate the possibility of chain reaction on March 3, 1940. He wrote about this successful experiment:

> . . . everything was ready and all we had to do was turn a switch, lean back and watch the screen of a television tube.
>
> If flashes of light appeared on the screen, that would mean that neutrons were emitted in the fission process of uranium and this, in turn, would mean that the large-scale liberation of atomic energy was just around the corner.
>
> We turned the switch and we saw the flashes.
>
> We watched them for a little while and then we switched everything off and went home.
>
> That night there was little doubt in my mind that the world was headed for grief.

Similar experiments performed by Fermi at Columbia and the Joliot-Curie team in Paris confirmed the fact that, while there were many problems to be solved, nuclear reaction was possible.

The most apparent problem was going to be separating the light uranium-235 from heavier uranium-238. Both are found in uranium ore, and U-235 is different only because it contains three fewer neutrons in its nucleus. Only the U-235 is fissionable, and it makes up only 0.7 percent of ordinary U-238. If the heavier U-238 was bombarded, its nucleus might catch and trap the neutron instead of splitting it. Since the lighter U-235 was such a small part of uranium ore, the possibility of separating enough to produce a bomb seemed remote in 1939 and 1940.

There was an apparatus known as a mass spectrometer that could separate small amounts, but it would have required twenty-seven million spectrometers to produce one kilogram of U-235 a year, In the early days of atomic work, the apparent stumbling block would be getting enough U-235.

British scientists were considering the gaseous-diffusion method of uranium separation in 1939. It was based on a principle called Graham's law, that stated if two gases, one lighter than the other, are passed through a porous medium, the lighter gas will eventually separate. Since U-235 was lighter than U-238, the method might be used to separate out the fissionable U-235. This method would be used later in Oak Ridge, Tennessee, but in 1940, the scientists working in the United States were not considering this possible solution.

Despite the obvious problems, groups of scientists began to push for a concerted effort to develop atomic weapons immediately after the Hahn-Strassman experiment became known. Leo Szilard, who led in the voluntary secrecy action, was also one of the first to begin to lobby for the support of the United States government. On March 16, 1939, the day Hitler annexed Czechoslovakia, Enrico Fermi delivered a letter to the chief of the United States naval operations telling him about the experiments going on at Columbia University.

Since none of the group of scientists was a citizen, it was

difficult for them to get the attention they needed to be heard and taken seriously. One story is that Fermi never got in to see the chief but told his story to two junior officers. They listened to his heavy Italian accent, his scientific talk about atomic fission, bombs, and submarines, and, when he left, one said to the other, "That guy is crazy!"

The foreign scientists were frustrated by what they saw happening in Europe. Uranium ore, which was essential for atomic work, had come from Czechoslovakia. Now that Hitler had overrun that small country, it was no longer available. The only other source of the ore known at that time was the Belgian Congo. What would happen if Belgium and consequently its African colony were taken by enemy forces?

Szilard and four other scientists visited the most famous physicist of them all, Albert Einstein, and begged him to help them. Though he had developed the theory of relativity, the possibility of a chain reaction and the use of atom splitting as a weapon had not occurred to him. Nevertheless, he was convinced it was a logical possibility. It was decided that their best chance to be heard would be if Einstein wrote to President Roosevelt.

Szilard, Teller, and Alexander Sachs actually wrote the letter, but Albert Einstein signed it. It said, in part:

> . . . it may become possible to set up a nuclear chain reaction in a large mass of uranium by which vast amounts of power . . . would be generated . . .
>
> This new phenomenon would also lead to the construction of bombs . . .

The letter was delivered on October 11, 1939, just one month after Hitler had invaded Poland, bringing a declaration of war from Great Britain and France. President Roosevelt moved swiftly, setting up an advisory committee to determine whether the Belgians would supply uranium ore deposits from the Belgian Congo. This was the immediate problem, since in 1939, in all of the United States, there was less than an ounce of metallic uranium.

As a result of this effort, 1,200 tons (1,089 m t) of uranium ore were shipped to the United States from the Belgian Congo in August 1940. The shipment was just in time, for at that very moment, Belgium was being overrun by the Nazis.

Since the United States was not at war, there was little further action taken in support of atomic research for several months. However, scientists continued to work as rapidly as they could. Early in 1940, the United States government awarded its first grant for atomic research—$6,000 to Columbia University. That was a modest beginning for a project that would soon require billions.

The problem of separating the fissionable U-235 from U-238 seemed insurmountable until experiments by Niels Bohr and John Wheeler in Denmark suggested that only under certain conditions could U-238 dampen the chain reaction qualities of U-235. It appeared that if the neutron "bullets" used to bombard the atom could be slowed down to speeds of no more that one mile per second, the U-238 nucleus could not steal them and prevent the chain reaction of the U-235 atom.

In order to slow down the neutrons and attempt chain reaction, Fermi, Szilard, and others built a structure of bricks and uranium and graphite with the $6,000 grant at Columbia University. Later, the whole effort was moved to the University of Chicago and given the code name "Metallurgical Laboratory."

It was on a squash court at the University of Chicago on December 2, 1942, that the first self-perpetuating chain reaction actually took place. The structure of bricks of uranium and graphite was the first atomic furnace, or pile, and it ignited the first atomic fire. It was, of course, a small atomic explosion, and the scientists were terrified that they might not be able to keep it under control. The experiment was a complete success and the atomic fire was allowed to burn for twenty-eight minutes. One year after the United States

Artist Gary Sheahan painted this picture of Enrico Fermi and the team of scientists who constructed the first atomic pile and created the first atomic chain reaction on a squash court at the University of Chicago.

entered World War II, the first chain reaction had been achieved.

While Fermi and his group of scientists were working furiously at Columbia University and the University of Chicago, other scientists were working just as energetically in other parts of the nation and world. Scientists at the University of California at Berkeley discovered plutonium in 1940. There was hope that it might be produced in larger quantities and eliminate the necessity for going through the difficult process of extracting U-235 from uranium ore. However, plutonium was made from U-238 and large quantities of neutrons were needed. Since the only way to get the neutrons was by using U-235, plutonium did not completely solve the U-235 extraction problems.

These and other atomic efforts were under the direction of a new committee called the Office of Scientific Research and Development. In June 1940 President Roosevelt had appointed Vannevar Bush, president of Carnegie Institute, chairman, and he introduced the first formal security measures of the atomic project. He also added well-qualified scientific personnel to the uranium experimentation efforts.

In the early stages of the war, British scientists were even more enthusiastic about the possibilities of atomic research than the United States was. Great Britain's committee of top scientists issued the M.A.U.D. report in 1941. The M.A.U.D. Committee—which stood for Military Application of Uranium Detonation—concluded that building an atomic bomb was possible. It said it was not only possible but construction efforts should begin immediately because it might be the decisive weapon.

Based on the British report and the obvious possibility that the United States would soon be in the war, President Roosevelt appointed a new committee. Called the S-1 Committee, it was supposed to report back in six months and say whether or not building a bomb was really feasible. The committee was appointed on December 6, 1941. The next day, December 7, 1941, the Japanese attacked Pearl Harbor, and the United States was at war. Six months later the S-1 Committee recommended a crash program, with a cost of more than $100 million, which, they said, might produce a bomb by July 1944.

Six months after that report, Enrico Fermi's group produced the famous chain reaction on the squash court at the University of Chicago. At exactly the same time that experiment was taking place, a conference was in session three blocks away that was to decide whether or not to attempt constructing plutonium plants. The successful demonstration of chain reaction settled the question and the atomic bomb push started in earnest. Until 1941 the total amount spent on atomic research by the United States government had been $300,000. In just two years, from 1943 to 1945, more than $2 billion would be spent.

Scientists in the United States would work day and night to develop the atom bomb before the Germans could. The nearly three years that followed the experiment on the squash court were a period of intense effort and secrecy. A curtain of absolute silence was drawn between the atomic scientists and the rest of the world, and the race was on!

CHAPTER IV

THE MANHATTAN PROJECT

The Manhattan Project, officially called the Manhattan Engineer District, was formed by President Roosevelt in June 1942. President Roosevelt appointed Brigadier General Leslie R. Groves to direct the project.

Groves had a reputation for getting a task accomplished, and though he sometimes irritated and offended people he worked with, he was a logical choice for the job. He was a graduate of West Point and an engineer whose previous assignment was deputy chief of construction for the Army Corps of Engineers. When he received the appointment, he was in his mid-forties and looking forward to an overseas assignment. Though he'd been in the Army since he graduated from West Point in 1918, he'd never been in battle. He was disappointed to find he would not be sent overseas, but he quickly took command of the Manhattan Project, instituting much tighter security measures immediately.

It was Major General Wilhelm D. Styer who told him of the appointment. Groves remembers that he said,

> Groves, you've been personally selected for this job by the Secretary of War, and the President has approved. The Project is in good shape—research and development are already done. Your job will just be to put the rough designs into final shape, build

some plants, and organize an operating force and your job will be finished and the war will be over.

Of course, this was a gross overstatement of the actual state of research and development. And although Styer's prediction that the atom bomb would end the war turned out to be correct, in 1942 there was no way of guessing that the atom bomb could even be built.

Within three days of beginning his new job, Groves said he was aware of the enormous challenges he faced. Far from being in good shape, the atomic project was in almost total confusion. There were experiments going on in several laboratories scattered over several university campuses. The American scientists and European refugees who were working on atomic energy experiments had only informal ways of keeping abreast of each others' experimental work. There was also a great deal of work being done in Canada and England, but little coordination between scientists in Allied countries and the United States. Instead of the efficient beginnings that Groves had been promised, it was clear that the enterprise was confused and scattered.

What's more, the research was nowhere near the level of completion that he had been told. Scientists were not certain they could build an atomic bomb at all. Uranium was very scarce and desperately needed if the bomb was to be constructed. There was not even agreement about how to proceed with the construction. The basic research was not done, and, even though there was a theoretical basis for the use of atomic fission to produce tremendous energy, if a practical method of chain reaction could be found, scientists were not certain it would actually be possible to build an atomic bomb. What's more, even if the atom bomb was possible, there was a great deal of confusion about what method of producing atomic fission was most practical.

Scientists knew that atomic fission and probably chain reaction could be achieved by using either uranium (U-235) or plutonium (Pu-239), but they were not sure which was the best approach. There were many people in several different facilities working on various aspects of the problem and opinions varied a great deal. General Groves had to sift through a lot of conflicting research, opinions, and facts in order to decide which method would develop an atomic weapon fastest and most efficiently.

At the time he took over, the possibility of building an atomic bomb was still debatable. While it was known that plutonium could be produced in an atomic reactor, it was not clear whether that would be a practical method of building a bomb. If uranium was to be used as the basis of a bomb, there were many different opinions about the best way to separate the indispensable U-235 from the uranium ore. Some scientists believed that it would be better to concentrate on building a plutonium bomb, others believed uranium would be more efficiently produced.

Ten weeks after Groves was appointed, Enrico Fermi demonstrated that chain reaction was actually possible. The news made the whole project more feasible but there were still many who doubted the practicality of the Manhattan Project. General Groves ignored all objections, visited several research centers, and talked with many scientists. After a few weeks of initial investigations, Groves decided he could not afford to wait and see whether one method would prove more practical and economical than another. He ordered a crash effort for the U-235 and Pu-239 systems. It would be costly but they would attempt to build bombs using both uranium and plutonium as fuel. It seemed to Groves that this was the best way to proceed, given the urgency of the situation and the indefinite state of atomic research in 1942.

Under General Groves's direction, the atomic effort was split up and spread across the United States. The first site selected was Oak Ridge, Tennessee, where the Army acquired fifty-four thousand acres of land and began immediate work constructing an "atomic city." In Oak Ridge, scientists would attempt to produce enough U-235 from uranium ore to build bombs.

The Oak Ridge site had all the necessary requirements

for an atomic plant: plenty of water, enough electricity, good roads, and a mild climate. Most important, it was in a totally isolated part of the country and tight security would be possible.

Building the Oak Ridge site was a tremendous engineering and architectural feat. The workers devised new construction methods and worked at such speed that, at one point, workers' houses were being constructed at a rate of one every two hours.

The final site included a gigantic half-mile long diffusion plant for the purpose of separating U-235 from uranium ore. In that plant, there were three million feet of corrosion-proof piping. There were many other plants and houses for workers, and construction activity was tremendous.

The whole project had to be kept secret. Local people speculated about the amount of activity, but the security was so tight that some people working in one office didn't know what others down the hall were doing.

All the way across the country, in Hanford, Washington, a plant to produce plutonium was constructed. The site was selected in January 1943, and within a few months forty-five thousand workers were building "plutonium city." At the beginning of the war, scientists were producing plutonium at the impossibly slow rate of a kilogram every twenty thousand years. By 1943 the Hanford plant was producing plutonium in amounts large enough to build three bombs.

There were other sites that were very important to the Manhattan Project. The University of California at Berkeley developed the electromagnetic process for separating U-235 from uranium ore. Columbia University in New York City was responsible for the development of a gaseous diffusion process for U-235 separation.

In Milwaukee, Wisconsin, the Allis-Chalmers Company was responsible for manufacturing pumps. In Detroit, Chrysler Corporation produced production diffusers, the containers in which the barriers used to separate the U-235 would be placed.

In Decatur, Georgia, the Houdaille-Hershey Corporation produced the actual barrier that was needed to separate the uranium. The barrier was one of the toughest problems facing the Manhattan Project, and for a time it appeared that no barrier could be designed that would hold up in industrial use. Those small experiments performed in university laboratories were a long way from the military manufacturing that the Manhattan Project demanded.

More than once, money and effort were committed to a phase of the design problem without any real assurance that the problems that preceded it would be solved. From 1943 until 1945, scientists worked full speed, at a rate they had not imagined possible. Seven-day weeks of ten- and twelve-hour days were normal.

Spreading the plants used in atomic bomb production all over the United States had two major advantages: safety and security. At the beginning, General Groves had considered putting the plutonium production plant at Oak Ridge, along with the uranium production, but he decided it was too dangerous. Losing a plant through accident or military attack was a possiblity, and if they were widely separated, the second facility would still be in existence. In addition, tremendous amounts of electrical power would be needed and the uranium production facility would also use great amounts of power. The second facility was placed elsewhere to avoid a power shortage.

Los Alamos, New Mexico, is perhaps the best-known site of the Manhattan Project because it was there that the bomb was actually designed, assembled, and tested. The first buildings on the Los Alamos site were actually dormitories of a boys' school called the Los Alamos Ranch School. That was taken over by the Army, along with the fifty-four thousand acres that surrounded the school.

The Los Alamos site was very remote, and the road that led to the 7,300 foot (2,200 m) high plateau was narrow and steep. The scientists lived in dramatically difficult conditions or had to commute from Santa Fe or nearby ranch houses. In the beginning there was no cafeteria or cooking facilities.

Telephone service was bad, and often people had to drive into Santa Fe instead of talking on the phone. Some of the scientists and their families resented the strict military rules that surrounded their lives, yet security had to be maintained.

The security rules were very elaborate, and the setting was extremely remote. No one was allowed to cash a check in town or have a checking account in a local bank. Babies who were born at Los Alamos had only a post office box number on their birth certificates; weddings and deaths could not be announced in the newspaper. Some children were registered at school with no last names. Many scientists had to use false names, inside the plant as well as outside.

There was a lot of personal surveillance, too. Letters were steamed open by the security forces, telephone calls were monitored, outgoing letters had to be sent unsealed, and the censors read them and sent them back if they were "objectionable."

After one year of operation, the population of Los Alamos was more than six thousand, but it was never on the map and there was never a post office. Officially, it did not exist, though the Army called it Site Y. The tight security irked many of the workers and scientists attached to Los Alamos and other facilities, but it was under General Groves's command and basically successful. No word leaked to the Japanese or Germans about the work being done at Oak Ridge or Los Alamos.

J. Robert Oppenheimer was director at the Los Alamos site. Though an American, he had studied in Europe for years, and that was one reason why General Groves picked him for the job. He had a doctorate from the University of Göttingen in Germany and he had also studied in The Netherlands and at the Cavendish Laboratories in Great Britain. He knew many of the European scientists who worked with him on the project and commanded their respect.

Some of the most famous scientists in the world worked at Los Alamos at one time or another during the war years. They included the Americans, Marshall Holloway and Louis Slotin,

who would assemble the bomb, and William "Deacon" Parsons who would arm the bomb en route to Hiroshima. There were also many famous European scientists. Hungarians Edward Teller, Leo Szilard, John Wigner, and the mathematician John Von Neumann. James Chadwick and Rudolph Peierls came from England. German refugees included Otto Frisch and Klaus Fuchs. The Italian group was headed by Enrico Fermi and included Emilio Segré and Bruno Pontecorvo.

One of the biggest events in Los Alamos history was the arrival of Niels Bohr after he escaped from Denmark in 1943. He was a recognized leader of atomic scientists and well-loved because he had befriended many of the Europeans attached to the project. His appearance cheered the other scientists, and he immediately began counseling and advising on construction problems.

About the same time Bohr arrived from Denmark the first plutonium arrived from Hanford, Washington, and the first uranium arrived from Oak Ridge, Tennessee. Since the shortage of uranium and plutonium had been one of the most critical problems, the actual manufacture of some amount of the vital materials encouraged the scientists.

Nevertheless, life at Los Alamos continued to be discouraging and difficult. There were many problems between the military and civilian personnel. Many of the scientists' wives and children despised the primitive living quarters and the heat that could reach as high as 120 degrees. Open quarrels broke out between civilians and the military officers in charge of Los Alamos, mostly about living conditions. The need for secrecy provided reasons for tight control of scien-

J. Robert Oppenheimer, who directed scientific work at the Los Alamos, New Mexico, site of the Manhattan Project.

tific workers who were not in the military and some of them bitterly resented the restrictions. Scientists were forced to use false names, and they had guards constantly assigned to them to see that they obeyed security regulations. Sometimes civilian scientists, traveling with top-secret documents, had their briefcases chained to a security guard's wrist.

Not only were the scientists discouraged by the living conditions and strict military discipline at Los Alamos, but they were doubtful that they would be able to build a bomb fast enough to beat the Germans. And, indeed, there were so many different problems facing them it is remarkable that it was completed in such record time.

One problem they had to solve was how to transport plutonium from Hanford, Washington, to Los Alamos without having it explode on the way. They worked out a system where small amounts of plutonium were shipped in a thick jellylike solution inside wooden boxes so that it could not possibly explode, even if there were an accident.

The boxes containing plutonium were carried inside Army ambulances, and they were accompanied by military-police cars with guards. None of the men involved in the transporting knew what they were carrying except one officer who rode in the ambulance. Each time, the driver took a different route between Hanford and the drop-off point at Port Douglas, Utah. There, a Los Alamos ambulance would pick up the plutonium shipment and carry it into the plant. There were a couple of these trips a week once the Hanford plant began to produce plutonium.

Other problems were larger and at times threatened to destroy the whole bomb-building effort. The plutonium production plant in Hanford had cost three hundred fifty thousand million to build, but for a while it looked as though the whole effort was wasted. When the construction was completed and the scientists attempted to fire up the giant reactor, the chain reaction would not continue for any length of time. Within three and a half hours, the plant would shut down. Eventually, it was discovered that there were design problems and the solution was to put more uranium in the reactor.

The designers had not built that extra uranium capability into their plans and if the blueprints had been followed exactly as they came out of the Chicago Metallurgical Laboratory, the program would have failed. However, one engineer who was involved in the actual building of the plant had insisted on adding that extra uranium capacity—"just in case." His foresight earned him praise from fellow workers, and he was the subject of a ballad written by one of the construction workers that ended like this, "Regardless of his rank or state,/One man can sway a nation's fate."

Despite problems with production, the plutonium-based bomb looked more promising in the spring of 1944 than the original plan to produce a bomb based on U-235, extracted from uranium. There was a shortage of uranium ore and there was talk of abandoning the uranium project completely in favor of the plutonium-based bomb project. Eventually, scientists were able to separate enough U-235 from uranium ore to build one bomb, which was used at Hiroshima.

At Los Alamos, there were problems inherent in preparing to test the atomic weapons. The scientists discovered that the method of firing they had used in uranium atomic experiments would not work with plutonium. Since there was not going to be enough uranium for a test bomb, Los Alamos scientists were faced with a new problem for which there did not appear to be a solution.

In time, the scientists devised a way to fire the plutonium-based weapon using the principle of implosion. Implosion meant that pieces of plutonium would be blown together in a small ball by explosives that would push them from the outside toward the center. When the pieces of plutonium met, atomic explosion would result. The implosion process was very experimental, and there was some question whether scientists would ever be able to develop enough accuracy to control the results. In general, the scientists at Los Alamos mistrusted the method, but it was the only one possible.

John Von Neumann headed a group of more than six hundred people who worked on the implosion problem. Its solution was one of the biggest secrets of the whole atomic effort, and the procedures were still classified twenty-five years later. However, one of the workers on the problem was the British traitor, Klaus Fuchs. A German refugee who had become a British citizen, he was part of the group of British citizens who worked on the atomic bomb project at Los Alamos. In 1950 he would be arrested and convicted of espionage in his home country of Great Britain. It would be discovered that he had given the secret of implosion and much more information to the Soviet Union during the time he was working on atomic energy because he believed in communism as a form of government. The treason of Klaus Fuchs was not discovered until later, however, and work on the implosion problems continued uninterrupted.

Balanced against Fuchs' treason were people like Louis Slotin who were willing to risk their lives in order to win the race of atomic weapons. Slotin was a 33-year-old American scientist who performed the dangerous experiments called "tickling the dragon's tail" that were necessary for the development of the implosion method. An extremely brave man, Slotin took his life in his hands each time he dropped a small piece of fissionable material through the center of an assembly to produce a short-lived chain reaction.

Slotin would lose his life right after the end of World War II while he was performing the "dragon's tail" experiment. A screwdriver slipped from his hand and he covered the experimental equipment with his bare hands in order to protect the other scientists in the room from lethal doses of radioactivity. He died a few hours later.

The production of the atom bomb required the total dedication of many workers and a combination of foresight, luck, and caution. Cloaked in secrecy, guarded by the military, and dependent on the scientific expertise of some of the most brilliant scientists in the world, this weapon was constructed in the most remarkable crash program ever seen.

CHAPTER

TRUMAN BECOMES PRESIDENT IN A TROUBLED WORLD

The Manhattan Project was started under President Franklin Delano Roosevelt, and most of the research was completed under his leadership. Roosevelt received Albert Einstein's letter describing the possibility of constructing atomic weapons in 1939. That letter, actually written by Szilard, Teller, and Sachs, was the beginning of Roosevelt's shepherding of atomic research. From that time on, the president watched the growth of the atomic project from a small grant to Columbia University to a massive endeavor called the Manhattan Project. Although he was not a scientist himself, Roosevelt understood the significance and some of the construction concepts behind the atom bomb. He had also had time to adjust to its possible importance in the balance of world power.

Roosevelt was a man who was loved, respected, and hated for his dynamic programs and creative leadership. When he was reelected in 1944 for the fourth time, many people suspected his health was bad. By then, however, the United States had been at war for three years, and the voters felt it was the wrong time to change presidents.

Most people were hoping the tedious, difficult war would not drag on much longer; yet there was no way to predict exactly how long it would take to defeat the Germans and Japanese. Nevertheless, the winning countries were already discussing peacetime problems in the expectation that the war would soon be over.

Almost immediately after his fourth inauguration in January, 1945, Roosevelt went to Yalta, on the Black Sea, to meet with Prime Minister Winston Churchill of Great Britain and Marshall Joseph Stalin of the Soviet Union. Most historians date the Yalta Conference as the beginning of the Cold War between the United States and Russia.

Later, Stalin was quoted as saying,

> This war (World War II) is unlike all past wars. Whoever occupies a territory imposes his own social system. Everyone imposes his system as far as his army can advance.

The Russians apparently followed his statement as a plan of action, because every country that their troops took back from the Germans fell under Soviet control.

At Yalta, the three leaders—Churchill, Roosevelt, and Stalin—tried to make basic decisions about how the invasion of Europe would proceed, whose troops would liberate what countries. Roosevelt also sought Russia's support in the fight against Japan, a part of the conflict that the Soviet Union had so far avoided. Because Roosevelt knew neither how long it would take to defeat Japan nor whether an invasion of the Japanese mainland would be necessary, he felt very strongly that he needed Russian assistance in that fight.

In return for Russian support against Japan, Roosevelt agreed to terms that some historians feel helped create more tension between the two countries because it gave Russia too much power in world affairs. Those who defend Roosevelt point out that at the time of the Yalta Conference in February 1945, Roosevelt thought he needed Soviet help against the Japanese more than would actually be the case. Roosevelt did not know whether the experiments going on at Los Alamos would actually result in a workable bomb, and he assumed the Japanese mainland would have to be invaded.

Some feel he should have driven a tougher bargain with the Russians and blame him for the world problems that followed. Others insist that there were historical reasons for the animosity between the Russians and their American and British allies that were bound to erupt into Cold War.

Relations with Russia had always been complicated and were due to get worse. Until the spring of 1941, the Soviet Union had been an ally of Germany. From the middle of 1940, when France fell to Hitler's invading army, Great Britain had stood alone in the fight against Nazi Germany. In the spring of 1941, Hitler split his efforts against Great Britain by invading the Soviet Union, and that December, after Pearl Harbor, the United States entered the war against Germany as well as Japan.

From the time they entered the war, the United States leaders saw World War II as a war of weapons. Lacking the tremendous industrial capability of the United States, the Russians had been forced to fight their war with men in the infantry instead of depending on advanced weapons and machinery. Fierce battles raged on Russian soil, and the Soviet people suffered tremendous casualties. Part of the reason for the suspicion and mistrust of the Russian leaders for the British and Americans was that they had suffered such a high casualty rate.

The United States had also suffered great casualties but proportionately less than the European nations. At the same time, no country matched the tremendous industrial and manufacturing effort of the United States; the Manhattan Project was just one aspect of the race to produce weapons. Conventional weapons such as ships, planes, and bombs were built as fast as possible, but by 1945 the United States military leaders understood that the atom bomb might be the greatest weapon of all. The question of whether or not to tell the Soviet Union about the possible atomic weapon is typical of the complicated relationshp of the time. In the end, the atom bomb was not mentioned at Yalta, and it is unclear whether or not the Russians were given a true picture of the atomic weapon's significance at the later conference at Potsdam.

By the time of the Yalta Conference, relations were very strained between the United States and the Soviet Union. In retrospect, the fact that Klaus Fuchs was spying for the Soviet Union indicates how mistrustful the Allies really were of each other. And the fact that Roosevelt did not mention the possibility of having an atom bomb shows a lack of trust on both sides.

By the time the Yalta Conference ended in February 1945, American leaders were probably as concerned about the possible problems with Russia as with winning the war. Roosevelt was quite ill when he returned to the United States, and some historians feel his poor health at the Yalta Conference influenced his decisions and, therefore, the fate of the world. On his return, Roosevelt traveled to his retreat in Warm Springs, Georgia, to recuperate from the trip. On April 12, 1945, the president died.

At the time of his death, the work at Los Alamos and the other factories involved in atomic production was in full swing. Scientists were discussing dates and sites for the first atomic bomb test. The man who stepped into the presidency, Harry S. Truman, had never even heard of the atomic bomb.

During twelve of the thirteen years Roosevelt was president, Harry S. Truman had been the junior senator from Missouri, loyal to the president's New Deal policies. His selection as running mate for Roosevelt's campaign for a fourth term surprised most politicians. Some have suggested that the facts that Truman had talked to Roosevelt only twice since he had been elected and that Truman knew nothing about the atom bomb were signs that Roosevelt didn't have very high regard for him.

A more logical reason for Truman's ignorance is given by Secretary of State James F. Byrnes in his memoirs:

> I must say you have to understand it that President Roosevelt, I'm sure, just did not have the time to advise Mr. Truman, who had become Vice-President on January 20, of the Manhattan Project. You will

recall that forty-eight hours after Mr. Roosevelt was inaugurated for that term he went to Yalta. He was away for more than six weeks. When he returned he was sick and I know his illness which prevented him from doing anything more than was absolutely necessary was responsible for his not having advised Truman of the Manhattan Project.

Whatever the reason, President Truman's first news of the atomic bomb being developed at Los Alamos came a few minutes after he was sworn in as president. After the ceremony, Secretary of War Henry L. Stimson asked to speak to Truman about an urgent matter. Truman recalled the moment:

> Stimson told me that he wanted me to know about an immense project that was under way—a project looking to the development of a new explosive of almost unbelievable power. That was all he felt free to say and his statement left me puzzled. It was the first bit of information that had come to me about the atomic bomb but he gave me no details. It was not until the next day that I was told enough to give me some understanding of an almost incredible development that was under way and the awful power that might soon be placed in our hands.

Truman might have learned something of the Manhattan Project several months earlier if he had not been diverted from his efforts. As chairman of a Senate committee to investigate

Harry S. Truman is sworn in as president on April 13, 1945.

war expenditures and possible waste, he had tried to visit the mammoth plant at Oak Ridge, Tennessee. When he and his committee were turned away at the gate, Truman complained. Secretary of War Stimson called him in and promised him that the expenditures he'd heard about were very necessary and that any investigation would endanger national security. Truman had believed him and stopped that aspect of the investigation. Not long after, he was running for vice-president.

Despite the fact that he had no previous information, Truman was immediately responsible for decisions about the development and use of the atomic bomb. He picked up the reins of government and guided the nation to victory.

On April 16, the Monday after Roosevelt's death, President Truman spoke to a joint session of Congress, and he repeated the determination of the United States to gain an unqualified, unconditional surrender from Japan. He said,

> . . . both Germany and Japan can be certain beyond a shadow of a doubt that America will continue to fight for freedom until no vestige of resistance remains. Our demand has been, and it remains, unconditional surrender. We will have no traffic with the breakers of the peace on the terms of the peace . . . America will never become a party to any plan for partial victory.

Germany was clearly defeated when Truman came to power. It surrendered unconditionally three weeks later, on May 7. When Truman took office, he recalled that his advisers had told him the probable timetable for defeating Germany was another six months. Their estimate for defeating Japan was a year and a half. Discussions about how to end the war with Japan continued to revolve around the possibility of an invasion. The atomic bomb was not often mentioned in those first days of Truman's administration, though scientists were working desperately to prepare a test of its effectiveness.

Truman was, however, soon told that the first uranium bomb would be ready for testing by August 1 and that a second plutonium bomb would be tested in July. He was also promised that another plutonium bomb would be available by the middle of August. While there was not absolute certainty that these promises could be fulfilled, they were fairly reliable predictions.

Shortly after the German surrender, President Truman began preparing to meet with Stalin and Churchill at Potsdam, Germany, to discuss the terms for Japanese surrender and other issues that were vital to the Allies. The conference was scheduled for July 15, and Truman and his advisors had to decide whether or not to tell the Soviet Union about the atomic bomb that was being developed. By then, relations between the Soviet Union and the United States were getting even more difficult.

Truman wrote in his memoirs that the ambassador to Russia, Averell Harriman, returned from Moscow to brief him. Truman remembered that Harriman was very worried about the Russians.

> (Harriman) said that in his judgment we were faced with a 'barbarian invasion of Europe' . . . He added that he was not pessimistic, for he felt it was possible to arrive at a workable basis with the Russians. He believed this would require a reconsideration of our policy and the abandonment of any illusion that the Soviet government was likely soon to act in accordance with the principles to which the rest of the world held in international affairs . . . I ended the meeting by saying, 'I intend to be firm in my dealings with the Soviet government.'

As Truman prepared to go to the Potsdam Conference, he had many questions to ponder; one of the most important was whether or not the atom bomb would actually work. The first test was scheduled soon, probably on the first or second day of the conference. If the bomb worked, should Russia be told about it? And was it still necessary for Russia to enter into the war against Japan, or would we be able to win without the Soviet Union?

The question of the Soviet Union's involvement in ending the war with Japan had tremendous impact on the future of China. China, which had been involved in a civil war, was fighting against Japan. Once the war was over, who would rule the Chinese mainland? The Chinese communists, as the Russians would like, or the old government under the leadership of Chiang Kai-shek? The politics at Potsdam were as complicated as the blueprint for design of any secret weapon. They were also potentially as deadly.

Truman went to Potsdam not knowing for certain that the atomic bomb was really going to work. Until that information was his, he could not decide how to treat the Russians and their demands for more territory in Europe. Nor could he know exactly how to define the words "unconditional surrender," and what demands to present to the Japanese. Many decisions rode on the completion of the atomic test at the Trinity site.

CHAPTER VI

TRINITY

The code name of the atomic bomb test was to be Trinity. The test was planned for some time around July 15. For some of the scientists, it seemed as though it was already too late. Germany had surrendered and the dreadful news that six million Jews had been deliberately exterminated in death camps was being published. The world reeled at the realization of how cruel humans could be to each other.

Scientists who had worked desperately to beat the hated Nazis now knew that the Germans had never come close to winning the atomic race, probably because Hitler had pulled scientists and money away from the atomic projects to work on the V-2 rockets, which Hitler believed would be the key to German victory. Though the Germans had continued to work on atomic research, they had not put forth the same determined effort as the United States.

But even though the Allies had defeated the Germans without the atom bomb, the war against Japan was still raging, and scientists and military leaders were ready to test the weapon that had been the object of the most tremendous effort of money and scientific intelligence in the history of mankind. J. Robert Oppenheimer, director of the Los Alamos site, wired two scientists who were invited to the test to let them know it would be soon. Because the test was so secret, he used a code name, "fishing trip," for the code name, Trinity. His wire said:

> Any time around the fifteenth would be good for our fishing trip. Because we are not certain of the weather, we may be delayed several days. We do not have enough sleeping bags to go around so we ask you please not to bring anyone with you.

The test was a secret, as was the whole Manhattan Project, of course, but one reporter, William L. Laurence, the science editor for *The New York Times*, was invited to view the test. Laurence had to agree that he would not write anything until after the end of the war. In the meantime, however, he had to explain his long absence to his bosses at the *Times* without disclosing what he would be covering or where he would be going. He said to them:

> The story is much bigger than I could imagine, fantastic, bizarre, fascinating, and terrifying. When it breaks it will be an eighth-day wonder, a sort of Second Coming of Christ yarn . . . It will need about twenty columns on the day it breaks.

It was not the first time Laurence had been allowed to visit the Los Alamos facility. At the government's invitation, he had been allowed inside in May 1945. The visit explained one of the mysteries Laurence had questioned during the war. Finally, he knew where scientific geniuses such as Enrico Fermi had disappeared. He recalls that when he ran into Fermi at Los Alamos, the scientist burst into laughter, ". . . the laughter of a child playing hide-and-seek who finds himself finally discovered."

The site chosen for the atomic test was on the Alamogordo Bombing and Gunnery Range about two hundred miles south of Los Alamos. It was owned by the Army and was one of the most remote places in the United States, so it seemed perfect. The bomb was placed inside an iron shed, on top of a 100-foot (30-m) steel tower. That spot was called ground zero. About 10,000 feet (3,048 m) from ground zero, Army engineers built concrete bunkers in all four directions. Inside those bunkers the scientists placed cameras and instruments to record the impact of the blast. The base camp for engineers, military personnel, and scientists was 10 miles (16 km) from ground zero.

As the test drew near, nerves grew shakier. Scientists were not sure how to predict the force of the bomb, and press releases were prepared to explain several possible results of the testing. General Groves called reporter Laurence into his office and asked him to write statements to cover the following possibilities.

1. A loud explosion was reported today. There was no property damage or loss of life.

2. An extraordinary loud explosion was reported today. There was some property damage but no loss of life.

3. A violent explosion occurred today, resulting in considerable property damage and some loss of life.

4. A mammoth explosion today resulted in widespread destruction of property and a great loss of life.

Even though the test was scheduled for July 16, Oppenheimer tried desperately to get an extension from General Groves as the scheduled date drew near. There were many problems to be solved, including troubles with the wiring at the Trinity test site. He wanted extra days to solve the technical problems, but General Groves gave him a definite no. On the other end, politicians in Washington were urging that the test be set forward. General Groves refused them as well.

General Groves's ability to say no to both scientists and

politicians was what made him the competent supervisor that he was. Under a weaker administrator, there is no doubt that the project would have foundered. He was not always well liked, and he had earned a reputation as a stubborn and demanding administrator. But he also had a reputation as a phenomenal worker. His stamina and unstinting energy made it possible to demand a lot from the scientists and military personnel working under him. Typically, Groves began his day at 8:30 A.M. and stayed at his desk until after midnight.

Groves was the leader who insisted the test be made on schedule, hewing to the primary purpose of seeing if the atom bomb would actually work. There were scientific instruments to measure the explosion and recording equipment for later observations, but no real attempt was made to measure the effects of an atomic explosion on humans. Some scientists suggested building structures with "dummy" humans or some live guinea pigs inside, but General Groves felt that it would be a waste of time and would possibly jeopardize security.

There were military medical personnel assigned to Los Alamos to assist in test preparations, but the scientists seemed to resent their interference. Since so little was known about the effects of radiation at that time, their precautions seem inadequate in retrospect. Nevertheless, the medical people had to fight the scientists to institute even the most rudimentary precautions. Worrying that the glare from the explosion might damage eyes, the medical men issued welders' dark goggles to prevent burning of retinas. They also set a radiation exposure limit of 5 roentgens for all personnel. By today's standards, that was dangerously high, but scientists and doctors did not know that in 1945. Some scientists wanted to roam about the test site freely immediately after the explosion, and they demanded radiation exposure limits of 25 to 50 roentgens—a truly reckless figure. The physicians, whose job it was to plan for possible disastrous aftereffects, were particularly worried and pessimistic about the results of Trinity and had several evacuation plans ready.

Though the test site was 30 miles (48 km) from the nearest town of Carrizozo, which had fifteen hundred people, no one could predict the exact intensity of the bomb. There was fear that the wind might suddenly shift and expose scientists and the citizens of nearby New Mexican towns to radioactive clouds.

During the sensitive period just before the testing, morale among the scientists and other workers was very important. Some scientists were extremely fearful of the results of the test and began to talk about the probability of disaster. Their predictions included the possibility of starting a chain reaction that would mean the end of the world. At the decision of Chief Medical Officer Stafford Warren, who acted as camp psychologist, some scientists were banished from camp because of the effect their fears were having on the others.

Another group of worriers was the weather people. It was very important for them to be able to predict the winds accurately since the atomic fallout could create havoc if it landed on a populated area. Predictions of the weather depended on one of the first computers in the nation; a giant machine sorted computer cards and compared weather conditions for more than forty years. Meteorologists selected July 28, 1900, as the day most like the forthcoming July 16 in terms of weather conditions. Using this date as a basis for their predictions, they pored over all the records and maps that were available. They wanted to make accurate predictions about weather conditions on the test date, especially concerning possible wind shifts, since the radioactive cloud that would follow the test would be lethal.

Other preparations for the test were equally complete and cautious. On July 2 a model of the plutonium assembly was driven over bumpy desert roads to determine how the bomb would hold up in transporting. On July 8 the explosives that would be used to ignite the bomb went through a trial assembly; each stage of the final test was checked as thoroughly as possible.

One check brought discouraging results. Two days

before Trinity, the bomb's firing circuits were tested but no explosion occurred. The scientists involved discovered that the detonation device had been prematurely discharged by a thunder shower earlier in the day. They realized that if it had been a real situation, the same thing would have happened, and the bomb test would have been a failure.

The failure of the firing circuits dismayed Oppenheimer and his colleagues. Two days before the test, many of the scientists at the Trinity site were so uncertain about the outcome of the tests that they were betting the test would fail or that the actual power of the explosion would be very small. Many scientists were full of foreboding and fear because so much depended on the success of the test, and they simply were not sure what to expect.

The test was scheduled for four o'clock in the morning on July 16, but a damp morning sky—or what might be called a light rain—postponed the test. No one wanted to delay the test if it could be avoided, but rain meant trouble. It could ruin electrical connections, and, even more important, a heavy rain could bring down excessive radioactivity in unpredictable ways. General Groves was worried about the town of Amarillo, Texas, 300 miles (483 km) to the southeast. If a rainstorm were to carry the fallout there, the seventy thousand inhabitants could not be evacuated.

Balanced by the fear of the rain, there was real pressure to test on July 16. Given the general pessimism of the work force, a delay or postponement might demoralize the Los Alamos scientists even more. By now, many of the scientists were so keyed up and fearful that they were calling for a halt to the testing, or predicting dire results. The most pressing reason, however, was political. Already, President Truman was in Potsdam, Germany, meeting with Stalin and Churchill. Knowledge of whether the United States had an atomic weapon was crucial to negotiations with the Russians.

General Groves, who understood the political necessity for the test, was the man who had the final decision. The test was delayed, when at the scheduled time of 4 AM the sky wasn't clear, but no one went home. At 5 AM, it was apparent

that the storm was over and the test would be performed, but an hour and a half late.

At 5:29 AM, the light flashed and the desert turned white with so brilliant a light that it made floodlights look pale. The responses of the men at the base camp ten miles away were varied. Some buried their heads or jumped into the sand to seek shelter. Others stood transfixed and remembered poetry. Oppenheimer thought of the sacred Hindu epic, and the stanza he later quoted became well known to Americans:

If the radiance of a thousand suns
Were to burst at once into the sky,
That would be like the splendor of the Mighty One . . .

I am become Death,
The shatterer of worlds.

Oppenheimer had lost forty pounds in the months preceding the test, and on the day of Trinity he weighed 120 pounds, remarkably light for a person more than six feet tall. Obviously, he was reacting greatly to the responsibility he felt for having been the leader of the atom bomb construction. In the days that followed, he would examine his efforts and publicly renounce his part in the work. But that morning he recalls that, like the other scientists there, he felt only elation that the bomb actually worked.

One soldier who was present heard another soldier say, "Buddy, you just saw the end of the war."

J. Robert Oppenheimer and Manhattan Project Director, General Leslie R. Groves, inspect the remains of the tower from which the Trinity test bomb was suspended.

Scientists passed drinks around to celebrate and General Groves said, "The war is over as soon as we drop two of these." Soon after that, he called his secretary and gave the code message to say the atom bomb test was a success. She in turn, called Potsdam, Germany, and the message was relayed to President Truman.

William Laurence of *The New York Times* viewed the test from 20 miles (32 km) away. He wrote the following description of the explosion that was the equivalent of 20,000 tons (18,000 m t) of TNT:

> Just at that instant there rose as if from the bowels of the earth a light not of this world, the light of many suns in one. It was sunrise such as the world had never seen, a great green supersun climbing in a fraction of a second to a height of more than eight thousand feet, rising ever higher until it touched the clouds . . .
>
> Up it went, a great ball of fire about a mile in diameter, changing colors as it kept shooting upward, from deep purple to orange . . . an elemental force freed from its bonds after being chained for billions of years . . . It was as though the earth had opened and the skies had split.
>
> Then out of the great silence came a mighty thunder . . . the first cry of a newborn world.

While Laurence intended to print his description after the war, there were other reporters who thought they had a story that day. The people living in the area heard and saw the explosion but had no idea what it was. Many of them called the newspapers to find out what had happened. Every police headquarters and newspaper room in the area was besieged by calls, and most newspapers tried to follow up on the story. The prepared news release was issued, supposedly from the commanding officer of the Alamogordo air base. It began this way:

An aerial view of the atomic bomb test site near Alamogordo, New Mexico, shows the shallow crater dug by the blast.

> An ammunition magazine, containing high explosives and pyrotechnics, exploded early today in a remote area of the Alamogordo air base reservation, producing a brilliant flash and blast which were reported to have been observed as far away as Gallup (New Mexico), 235 miles northwest.

The news story went on to say it might be necessary to evacuate a few civilians from their homes if the weather conditions affecting the content of the gas shells made it desirable. The story was so well accepted that, while it made the front page of some local papers, *The New York Times* didn't even report the explosion.

There was worry about fallout, and there is still debate about exactly how much damage the radioactivity did to the surrounding countryside, animals, and people. At the time, it looked as though there had been no real fallout damage.

The coded telegram that was sent to Secretary of War Stimson reported results that were satisfactory and, in fact, that exceeded expectations. The next telegram that was sent to Potsdam was also in code. It said:

> Doctor has just returned most enthusiastic and confident that the Little Boy is as husky as his big brother. The light in his eyes discernible from here to Highold and I could have heard his screams from here to my farm.

The telegram confirmed the outcome of the test at Alamagordo and said in code that the bomb that would be used on Hiroshima was crossing the Pacific. It promised that it would be as powerful as the Trinity device that had been visible for 250 miles (402 km). There was no time wasted between the test at Alamogordo and getting the bomb in position to be used as a real and very deadly weapon against the Japanese. The question of whether or not to use it would be up to President Truman.

CHAPTER VII

THE DECISION TO USE THE BOMB

Potsdam, where the conference between the three top leaders—Truman, Churchill, and Stalin—would be held, was near Berlin, the capital of Germany. The conference officially began on July 17 and lasted until August 2, 1945. President Truman made a tour of Berlin the day before the conference to see first hand what the damage from World War II was. He later wrote, "I saw evidence of a great world tragedy and I was thankful that the United States had been spared the unbelievable devastation of this war." The Germans had been totally defeated, and the city and country were in ruins. Hitler was dead and his followers would be tried in courts of law. In Europe the task of rebuilding was beginning.

But the Japanese were still fighting fiercely, and no one was sure how long they would hold out. Secretary of War Stimson wrote in a memoradum to Truman, "The Japanese soldier has proved himself capable of a suicidal, last-ditch defense; and will no doubt continue to display such a defense of his homeland." In that July 16 memorandum, Stimson went on to suggest that the time was ripe to warn Japan and if they continued to resist,

> the full force of our newer weapons should be brought to bear in the course of which a renewed

A kamikaze plane plummets to the ocean after being hit by antiaircraft fire before it could strike this U.S. carrier.

and even heavier warning, backed by the power of new forces and possibly the actual entrance of the Russians in the war, should be delivered.

Though it was clear that Japan would eventually be defeated, it looked as though the war might drag on for years and cost many thousands more American and Japanese lives. The battles raging on the islands of the South Pacific were fierce, and Japanese kamikaze pilots, though doomed to defeat, were a terrible weapon. The kamikaze planes, loaded with 250 to 550 pounds (113 to 249 kg) of TNT, would crash into targets in desperate suicide attempts to turn back the inevitable Japanese defeat. But despite Japan's persistence, the United States was taking islands, one by one. In February 1945 the United States conquered Iwo Jima, and in June the Marines finally took Okinawa, but the cost was horrifying. Japanese casualties at Okinawa were 109,629 killed and 7,871 taken prisoner. For the Americans, it was the heaviest casualty list of all the Pacific conquests: 12,520 killed and missing and 36,631 wounded.

The South Pacific victories assured the eventual defeat of Japan, but military leaders dreaded the proposed invasion of the Japanese mainland that was scheduled for November 1945. Stimson and other leaders hoped that warning the Japanese about newer weapons would avoid the need for a full-scale invasion of Japan.

Stimson and other American leaders were concerned about the timing of a warning to Japan, the entry of the Russians into the war against the Japanese, and future relations with the Russians. But, like most of the other leaders, Stimson's primary concern was for the quickest possible end to the war.

It is difficult to judge how eager the nation's leaders really were to have Russia enter the war against Japan, either before or after news of the atom bomb test arrived. Secretary of War Stimson and Secretary of State Byrnes have been quoted as saying they no longer felt it was of the utmost importance. Byrnes said:

> . . . Russia had said that after ninety days (dating from the Yalta Agreement) that she would enter the war but they [the Russians] had changed their minds before about things of that kind . . . Neither the President nor I were anxious to have them enter the war after we had learned of this successful test.

Secretary of War Stimson was in agreement:

> The news from Alamogordo . . . made it clear to the Americans that further diplomatic efforts to bring the Russians into the Pacific war were largely pointless. The bomb as a mere probable weapon had seemed a weak reed on which to rely, but the bomb as a colossal reality was very different. The Russians may well have been disturbed to find that President Truman was rather losing his interest in knowing the exact date on which they would come into the war.

However, President Truman, in his memoirs, says the following:

> There were many reasons for going to Potsdam, but the most urgent, to my mind, was to get from Stalin a personal reaffirmation of Russia's entry into the war against Japan, a matter which our military chiefs were most anxious to clinch.

It was to secure Russia's entry into the war against Japan that Roosevelt had agreed to many concessions during the Yalta Conference. Now the situation was changing; an invasion of the Japanese mainland might not be necessary. Earlier, having Russian troops attack Japanese forces in China would have been a good diversion and a way of sapping some of Japan's strength. But with the successful atom bomb test, it now looked as though the Japanese could be defeated without heavy losses of American troops. Even more than before, Churchill and Truman, with their advisers, had to consider whether Russian troops invading the Chinese Province of Manchuria would be a real help. If the atomic bomb was effective, there was no need to have the Russians invade Manchuria. And there was always the possibility that a Russian invasion might mean communist rule after the war.

The success of the Trinity test changed the United States' negotiating strength with the Russians after they arrived at Potsdam. By July 24, the prime minister of Great Britain, Winston Churchill, wrote: "It is quite clear that the United States do not at the present time desire Russian participation in the war against Japan."

Along with the United States, Great Britain also preferred that the Russians stay out of the war with Japan. However, the two countries could not protest if the Russians decided to keep their original bargain made at Yalta. Russian troops were lining up on the Manchurian border, preparing to invade China, and at the same time Russian officials were acting as intermediaries as the Japanese made tentative attempts to sue for peace.

On July 17 Stalin disclosed Japanese peace feelers to Churchill. The foreign minister of Japan, Shigenori Togo, sent word to the Japanese ambassador to Moscow, Naotaki Sato, that he was seeking peace. The conditions he sought included recognition of the Japanese Emperor. The message said in part:

> . . . if only the United States and Great Britain would recognize Japan's honor and existence we would terminate the war and would like to save mankind from the ravages of war, but if the enemy insists on unconditional surrender to the very end, then our country and His Majesty would unanimously resolve

to fight a war of resistance to the bitter end. Therefore, inviting the Soviet Union to mediate fairly does not include unconditional surrender; please understand this point in particular.

The Japanese did not know that the Russians had already agreed to enter the war against them. Some historians believe that if they had known, they might have appealed directly to the British or Americans, and peace might have been worked out sooner. However, they continued to seek help in negotiations from the Russians. (The last appointment of Ambassador Sato was with Foreign Minister Vyacheslav Molotov on August 8, two days after the atom bomb was dropped on Hiroshima. At that time, he was told that Russia was declaring war against Japan.)

At Potsdam, the three powers—the United States, Great Britain, and Russia—decided on a course of action in response to the Japanese peace overtures. Although they would continue to insist on unconditional surrender, originally the goal of all three countries, it was now Russia that was most insistent on holding the Japanese to that requirement, probably because they wanted to prolong the war long enough to invade Manchurian China. Not all U.S. leaders were totally against the idea of having the Emperor of Japan remain, but the United States ignored the peace feelers for other reasons.

When first told of the Japanese peace overture, Truman had replied, "I do not think the Japanese have any military honor after Pearl Harbor." Probably, Truman was very reluctant to trust any peace probes coming from such a long-standing enemy. There was the additional problem of beginning any peace negotiations with Russia involved. Secretary of State Byrnes, especially, did not trust Russia's intentions in the Far East.

Stalin, for his part, was apparently reluctant to push peace negotiations at that time because the Soviet Union would be in a position of more strength after the troops had

The opening meeting of the Potsdam Conference. President Truman is seated with his back to the camera; Marshal Joseph Stalin is at the right and Prime Minister Winston Churchill is on the left.

crossed the Manchurian border and the Russians were at war with Japan. So, although Japan's leaders did not know it, Japanese officials were asking the worst possible source for help in ending the fighting.

Whether the United States missed an opportunity to have peace without invading mainland Japan or using the atom bomb is a question that nags historians. Had the American leaders been so suspicious of both the Japanese and the Russians that they missed the significance of the peace feelers? Was Japan actually ready to talk about ending the war? If so, the question of whether or not the Emperor remained was solvable. In fact, there was some belief that the Emperor's influence would be needed to bring about peaceful surrender.

A great deal of thought went into wording the Potsdam Declaration, which was issued on July 26, 1945, especially the section on what the government of Japan would be like after World War II. The section was carefully worded, and though it called for unconditional surrender, it suggested that the Japanese had a right to choose their own form of government, presumably even keeping the Emperor, though no such possibility was specifically mentioned. The section, called paragraph 12, read as follows:

> The occupying forces of the Allies shall be withdrawn from Japan as soon as these objectives have been accomplished and there has been established in accordance with the freely expressed will of the Japanese people a peacefully inclined and responsible government.

Secretary of State Byrnes felt that the paragraph solved the problem of the Emperor by saying that the Japanese could decide for themselves. Other observers of Japanese culture feel that the paragraph made the acceptance of the Potsdam Declaration impossible. One of these observers was Eugene Dooman, special assistant to assistant secretary of state and an expert of Japanese affairs. He said of this paragraph in the Potsdam Declaration:

> The clause that was adopted, stipulating that a government should be established by the freely expressed will of the Japanese people, would transfer sovereignty from the Emperor, where it had reposed from time immemorial, to the Japanese people . . . It would be pointless to argue that, if the Japanese had been given the assurance that they could retain the Emperor, Japan would have surrendered without delay, thus making the (atom) bomb unnecessary. On the other hand, I think it could be convincingly argued that the denial of such assurances, along with the consequences of that condition that was laid down, namely, the transfer of sovereignty from the Emperor to the people, raised an issue of supreme importance to the Japanese requiring a reasonable length of time for a decision.

The Potsdam Declaration was a six-thousand word document dealing primarily with governing defeated Germany. It contained no warning of any special or terrible weapon, though it did promise "prompt and utter destruction" if the Japanese did not surrender immediately.

The reaction to the Potsdam Declaration within Japan was varied. By that time, it had become clear to many leaders that it was only a question of time before the Japanese would have to surrender. Foreign Minister Togo and Vice-Minister for Foreign Affairs Shunichi Matsumoto wanted to accept the document on the condition that the Emperor remain. Other, more militaristic, leaders felt that Japan should fight to the death. Debates began within Japan at the meeting of the Supreme War Council on July 27.

That same day, American planes dropped thousands of leaflets promising immediate and terrible bombings if the

Japanese did not surrender. Again, the atom bomb was not mentioned. The Japanese government answered the Potsdam Declaration with a statement that it would treat the declaration with *mokusatsu*, a Japanese word with many meanings ranging from "contempt" to "ignore." Much later, the prime minister said he meant it to be interpreted as "no comment" in English, but at the time both the American officials and the Japanese public thought it meant "beneath contempt." Whether or not the Japanese leaders really meant to flatly reject the Potsdam Declaration, their reply was interpreted as rejection.

The Potsdam Conference ended on August 2. By then it was accepted that the Japanese had definitely turned down the ultimatum calling for unconditional surrender, and many leaders, especially those who did not know of the atom bomb, expected the war to drag on for several more months.

During the conference, Truman and his aides had successfully deferred Russia's hopes that the United States formally request their entry into the war aginst the Japanese. Although it was expected that the Russians would enter the war sooner or later, Truman had withdrawn from Roosevelt's eager attitude at Yalta.

The Russians may or may not have actually known about the existence of the atom bomb at the close of the Potsdam Conference. According to Truman's memoirs, on July 24 he had "sauntered over to Stalin" and "casually mentioned" to him that "we had a new weapon of unusual destructive force." According to Truman,

> The Russian Premier showed no special interest. All he said was that he was glad to hear it and hoped we would make 'good use of it against the Japanese.'

Stalin may not have understood the import of Truman's message. Certainly, the American President did not intend to disclose any more than he felt was absolutely necessary to the

Soviet leader. Another reason that Stalin might not have shown more interest was that the atomic scientist, Klaus Fuchs, who was part of the British team working at Los Alamos, was relaying information to Russia by way of an accomplice. While Stalin probably hadn't received news of the successful atom bomb test, he may have known a great deal about the atomic bomb.

The English were kept better informed about the atomic bomb than the Russians. Since they'd been in on the original research work and had teams of scientists working at Los Alamos, they were partners in the bomb's development. Also, our basic relationship with Great Britain was much more trusting and stable than with the Russians. Churchill learned of the atom bomb almost immediately after Truman and he was delighted.

During the Potsdam Conference there was a recess so Churchill could return to Great Britain to face a general election. Churchill was defeated and replaced immediately by Prime Minister Clement Attlee who arrived soon after that July 26 election. On August 1, Truman wrote a letter to Attlee telling him about the atomic bomb. Attlee would later recall:

> In the light of what we knew at the time, which was that the military were in command in Japan and the Japanese would fight to their last man ... and the war would go on for six months, more probably ... with God knows how many casualties ... In the light of that, I figured the decision (to use the bomb) was right.

The decision to use the atomic bomb was made in many steps, beginning with Roosevelt's decision to fund research, and including the massive work effort put into the Manhattan Project. Some commentators feel that once the bomb was constructed and tested, there was no point at which the leaders of the United States could have turned back. President

Truman dated the final decision at July 25, when he signed an official directive to General Carl Spaatz, commanding general of the United States Army Strategic Air Forces, instructing him to drop the atomic weapon. The official order read:

> 1. The 509 Composite Group 20th Air Force will deliver its first special bomb as soon as weather will permit visual bombing after about 3 August, 1945, on one of the targets: Hiroshima, Kokura, Niigata and Nagasaki...
>
> 2. Additional bombs will be delivered on the above targets as soon as made ready by the project staff.

The attitudes of the leaders involved in the decisions were apparently unshaken. Winston Churchill later said, "The decision (at Potsdam) whether or not to use the atomic bomb was never an issue... (The) unanimous, automatic, unquestioned agreement represented a foregone conclusion."

And, Churchill restated more eloquently in his memoirs:

> To avert a vast indefinite butchery, to bring the war to an end, to give peace to the world, to lay healing hands upon its tortured peoples by a manifestation of overwhelming power at the cost of a few explosives seemed after all our toils and perils a miracle of deliverance.

President Truman, who was better known for his plain speech than for his eloquence, defended his decision in a different manner. He said, "Well, I'd say you question any young man who was over there and see what he thinks about it and he'll tell you off and he won't use polite language either."

Perhaps the most definite and clear statement came from General Groves who had this to say:

> As to my own position it was never in doubt, and that was that there was a war on; the mission had been given to me by Secretary Stimson through the development of atomic energy to bring the war to an end sooner than it would have otherwise ended and thus save American lives. No officer could possibly start to wonder should we use the weapon if we have it under such conditions . . . I said they could not fail to use this bomb because if they didn't use it that would have immediately cast a lot of reflection on Mr. Roosevelt and on the basis of that why did you spend all this money and all this effort and then when you got it, why didn't you use it? Also it would have come out sooner or later in a Congressional hearing if nowhere else just when we could have dropped the bomb if we didn't use it. And then knowing American politics, you know as well as I do that there would have been elections fought on the basis that every mother whose son was killed after such and such a date—the blood was on the head of the President.

While the use of the atomic bomb on the Japanese seemed unquestionable and even inevitable to many military and political leaders, there was a minority opinion, even among the military leaders. Admiral William Leahy opposed the use of the bomb as a military necessity. After the war, he wrote:

> It is my opinion that the use of this barbarous weapon at Hiroshima and Nagasaki was of no material assistance in our war against Japan. The Japanese were already defeated and were ready to surrender because of the effective sea blockade and the successful bombing of conventional weapons. It was my reaction that the scientists and others wanted to make this test because of the vast sums that had been spent on the project. Truman knew that and so did

the other people involved . . . My own feeling was that in being the first to use it we had adopted the ethical standards common to barbarians in the dark ages, I was not taught to make war in this fashion . . .

But the major resistance to using the bomb against the Japanese came from the scientists who were involved in the actual development of the weapon. Leo Szilard spearheaded an attempt by atomic scientists to persuade government leaders to warn Japan before using the bomb. The attempt began before the Trinity test with a document called the Franck Report. A group of scientists, including Szilard, James Franck, and Glenn Seaborg, who had worked in the Metallurgical Laboratory in Chicago as a part of the Manhattan Project, wrote a detailed statement opposing the use of atomic weapons against Japan. The Franck Report called for a demonstration of the bomb's power in "an appropriately uninhabited area," and pointed out that if we were to become involved in an arms race, the Russians could soon catch up.

After the Trinity test, there was another organized attempt by scientists to urge military and political leaders to reconsider their decision to use the bomb against Japan. On July 12, seventy-seven of the 150 atomic scientists working in the Metallurgical Laboratory in Chicago signed a petition that read in part:

> . . . the United States shall not resort to the use of atomic bombs in this war unless the terms which will be imposed upon Japan have been made public in detail and Japan, knowing these terms, has refused to surrender . . .

It is not clear exactly how much discussion about the use of the bomb was taking place at Los Alamos. Memories vary; Oppenheimer says there was little or none, while Teller remembers many discussions and a personal attempt to talk to the director, Oppenheimer, about what was happening in Chicago. No matter what the actual activity within Los Alamos was, no public statement came from the scientists.

It is probable that the opinion stated by Oppenheimer was representative of most of the scientists he headed. This opinion was based on intelligence reports that said Japan was prepared to fight on for many months. Oppenheimer fully endorsed the use of the bomb at that time.

> If it was needed to put an end to the war and had a chance of so doing, we thought that it the right thing to do.

The wheels were in motion, and many historians question whether any protest would have stopped them. President Truman had signed the official directive and targets were tentatively chosen. There was more indecision and uncertainty about whether the weather would be clear than about the decision itself. On August 5 the weather seemed right and the *Enola Gay* took off as planned.

The bomb that was dropped on Hiroshima was a uranium-based bomb. There were no others of that type available. However, there were three other plutonium-based bombs of the sort that had been tested at the Trinity site in New Mexico. They lay waiting for Japan's reaction to the first bomb. Would a second one be necessary to end the war?

If there is doubt about the necessity of dropping the first bomb, there is a great deal more doubt about dropping the second. Most especially, critics feel that the time between the first and second bombs was not long enough for the Japanese leaders to react. They were debating the possibility of surrender when news of the second bombing at Nagasaki arrived.

For a time the military leaders of Japan tried to keep the news of the utter destruction of Hiroshima secret. But by August 8, two days after the bombing, many political leaders understood the full impact of the special type bomb and were ready to react. Foreign Minister Tojo had an interview with the Emperor on August 8 and told him it was imperative to end the war. He recalls:

> The Emperor approved my view and warned that since we could no longer continue the struggle now that a weapon of this devastating power was used against us, we should not let the opportunity slip by engaging in attempts to gain more favorable conditions.

The Japanese also received news on August 8 that the Russians were entering the war against them. Yet, by American standards, they reacted slowly to the crushing blows. While the Supreme War Council of Japan was meeting in Tokyo to decide whether or not to surrender, the B-29 *Bock's Car* was flying toward Nagasaki.

Foreign Minister Tojo opened the council discussion by saying that the war was hopeless for Japan and surrender was necessary. He recalls the general reaction to his statement to the war council as being:

> All members of the Supreme Council already recognized the difficulties of going on with the war; and now, after the employment of atomic bomb and Russian entry into the war against us, none opposed in principle our acceptance of the [Potsdam] Declaration. None disagreed, either, that we must insist upon the preservation of the national policy as the indispensable condition of acceptance.

The Nagasaki bomb was dropped on August 9, and it broke a stalemate within the Japanese council that was debating surrender. Until that time, some military leaders had been holding out because their cultural training insisted Japan should fight to the end. The second bombing added belief to the

Nagasaki, after its destruction by the atomic bomb. Above: the towers of the Mitsubishi steel and arms works are all that remain of what had been the industrial heart of the city; Opposite: a Japanese man pushes his loaded bicycle along a path that has been cleared of rubble in this photograph taken about a month after the August 9th blast.

rumor that Tokyo would be bombed on August 12. The tradition of coming to consensus within the council before approaching the Emperor had to be broken. For the first time, Japanese leaders presented the problem directly to the Emperor, who listened to his top leaders for two hours. Finally, he decided that Japan must surrender.

The actual suit for peace and negotiations that followed took several days. The Japanese people learned of the cease-fire on August 15. For the victors and the vanquished, the problems of peace were now uppermost in mind. The war was over; the world had changed. Foremost among all changes was the dreadful new weapon, the atomic bomb. The world had entered the atomic age with a vengeance.

THE AFTERMATH

During and immediately after the surrender, there was a wave of suicides among Japanese military leaders. One top military leader, General Korechika Anami, typifies the attitude of the Japanese army leader's sense of failure. He committed suicide after news of the decision to surrender, leaving behind a bloodstained note apologizing:

> Believing firmly our sacred land shall never perish,
> I—with my death—humbly apologize to the Emperor
> for the great crime.

His great crime, of course, was losing the war. In the same frame of mind, there were kamikaze attacks on the American fleet that was sailing toward the Japanese mainland. There were many other suicides by military leaders and calls for a formal pact for a mass suicide.

The Japanese military code was a mixture of religion and cultural beliefs in pride. It baffled American soldiers—who had been taught that their first duty was to survive so they could fight another day—to see that Japanese soldiers preferred suicide over surrender. Officers routinely committed suicide rather than admit defeat and so did many of the regular soldiers. This attitude, taught early to the Japanese child, was that the only honorable alternative to victory was death and that surrender was so disgraceful it was unthinkable.

These beliefs, the suicides of Japanese soldiers, and the fact that Japanese soldiers who were left alone and out of communication on South Pacific islands continued to fight for as long as ten or twenty years, support the belief that until the atom bombings, the Japanese were prepared to fight to the death. Indeed, the Emperor spoke of the atom bomb when he explained his decision to surrender on the radio to his subjects.

> What is worse, the enemy, who has recently made use of an inhuman bomb, is incessantly subjecting innocent people to grievous wounds and massacre. The devastation is taking on incalculable proportions. To continue the war under these conditions would not only lead to annihilation of Our Nation, but the destruction of human civilization as well . . .

American troops occupied Japan after the war, and in 1946 the Emperor publicly renounced the idea that the Emperor is the same as God. That same year, the new Japanese constitution made him a "symbol of the state and the unity of the people." He could no longer take part in politics. But that represented almost no change. Until the fateful decision to surrender, the Emperor's part in Japanese politics had been basically symbolic. A compromise was reached that was satisfactory for most Japanese citizens and Americans.

The cities of Hiroshima and Nagasaki were eventually rebuilt. Today, Hiroshima is an important industrial city with one section set aside as a museum. This Peace Memorial Park was the site of the first annual world conference against nuclear weapons in 1955.

Since the end of World War II, Japan has consistently had a policy of peace, with little of its national budget spent for weapons. The nation spearheaded the anti-nuclear arms movement.

Japanese military and civilian dignitaries prepare to sign the surrender document aboard the U.S.S. Missouri. General Douglas MacArthur is at the far right.

In Hiroshima today, residents sit in Peace Park, opposite a cratered building that stands as a reminder of the destruction in 1945. To the left of the ruined building a new building is under construction, and to the right are the lights of a baseball park.

The use of atomic weapons against Japan has continued to be a controversial subject in the United States. Most of the leaders and scientists involved in the decision have spoken out on the subject. Their reactions vary from the insistence of the need for them by President Truman and General Groves to the revulsion expressed by Admiral Leahy. Views among the scientists involved are equally varied.

After the war, Leo Szilard actively protested the use of nuclear weapons and pressed for the peacetime use of nuclear power until his death in 1964. His colleague, Edward Teller, went on to become the scientist most closely associated with the development of the hydrogen bomb.

The hydrogen bomb was the subject of a major rupture among atomic scientists in the United States; the leaders of the two movements were Oppenheimer and Teller. After the war, Teller wanted to begin work immediately on the hydrogen bomb, a bigger and more powerful weapon based on splitting a hydrogen atom. In 1952 a hydrogen bomb exploded on the South Pacific island of Eniwetok was equivalent to 3 million tons (2.7 million mt) of TNT, proving Teller's statement that the atomic bomb was "obsolete" since the first atomic bomb was equal to 22,000 tons (20,000 mt) of TNT.

Oppenheimer, who cried when he heard the second bomb was dropped on Nagasaki, believed the hydrogen bomb should never be developed. Albert Einstein agreed with him, and the two scientists spoke out often on the subject of the danger of an arms race between Russia and the United States. Eventually, opposition to the hydrogen bomb broke out into an open and heated conflict between political and scientific leaders. In 1953 Oppenheimer was suspended from the Atomic Energy Commission as an alleged security risk, partly because of his opposition to the development of the hydrogen bomb. He continued to work at the Princeton Institute for Advanced Study until he died in 1967.

The United States did enter an arms race against Russia, and the Cold War, which had begun before World War II was over, continued to spur research and development of nuclear weapons. The Russians exploded their first atomic weapon in 1949, several years before United States leaders expected them to have the capability for construction of the weapon.

The mystery of Russia's unexpectedly speedy atomic development was partially explained when Klaus Fuchs, who had continued to work at the Atomic Research Station in Harwell, England, was caught and confessed to treason in January 1950. He spent several years in prison in England and then moved to East Germany in 1959.

In 1953 the Russians announced that they had exploded a hydrogen bomb. Since 1953 many nations have developed nuclear weapons, including Great Britain, France, and China. The fear of nuclear war has also spurred a strong peace movement in the United States, Japan, and many West European nations.

Debate over the use of the atomic bombs during World War II has tremendous import for a nation faced with decisions about the buildup of nuclear arms. In the forty years that followed the bombings of Hiroshima and Nagasaki, the tremendous potential for destruction that atomic fission started has been grasped. The greatest question facing humanity is whether we will use the new and terrible weapons to destroy the earth.

Reacting to just such a problem, Leo Szilard stated that "the world is headed for grief" when he first found a way to make chain reaction a reality. Since then, the question of how to avoid using the weapons that nations are developing is of primary importance. Japan has chosen not to enter the arms race, a move some critics say is possible because her chief protector, the United States, has been so deeply involved in the race for weapons buildup. Today, many people in many countries wonder if it is possible that the people who endured the primary impact of the atomic bomb have learned a lesson we must all learn in order to survive.

Albert Einstein wrote of this dilemma many times. In December 1955, the following statement appeared in the *Bulletin of Atomic Scientists*.

> There lies before us, if we choose, continual progress in happiness, knowledge, and wisdom. Shall we, instead, choose death, because we cannot forget our quarrels? We appeal, as human beings, to human beings: Remember your humanity and forget the rest. If you can do so, the way lies open to a new paradise; if you cannot, there lies before you the risk of universal death.

FOR FURTHER READING

BOOKS

Byrnes, James F. *Speaking Frankly*. New York: Harper and Brothers, 1947.

Churchill, Winston S. *The Second World War, Vol. 6, Triumph and Tragedy*. Boston: Houghton Mifflin, 1953.

Compton, Arthur H. *Atomic Quest: A Personal Narrative*. New York: Oxford, 1956.

Giovannitti, Len, and Fred Freed. *The Decision to Drop the Bomb*. New York: Coward McCann, 1965.

Groueff, Stéphane *Manhattan Project*. Boston: Little, Brown, 1967.

Groves, Lieut. Gen. Leslie R. *Now It Can Be Told*. New York: Harper and Row, 1962.

Lamont, Lansing. *Day of Trinity*. New York: Atheneum, 1965.

The New York Times. Hiroshima Plus 20. New York: Delacourt, 1965.

Sulzberger, C.L, and the editors of *American Heritage. The American Heritage Picture History of World War II*. New York: Crown, 1966.

Truman, Harry S. *Memoirs, Vol. 1, Year of Decisions*. New York: Doubleday, 1955.

MAGAZINE ARTICLES

"ABC's of Bomb Making," *Time*, June 22, 1981.

"Albert Einstein and the Bomb," *Saturday Review*, March 3, 1979.

Feld, Bernard T. "Einstein and the Politics of Nuclear Weapons," *Bulletin of Atom Scientists*, March 1979.

Moss, Norman. "Nuclear Power, the Promise and the Threat," *Illustrated London News*, April 1980.

Philips, John Aristotle, and David Michaelis. "How I Designed an A-bomb in My Junior Year at Princeton," *Esquire*, August 1, 1978.

Powers, Thomas. "Seeing the Light of Armageddon," *Rolling Stone*, April 10, 1982.

Rainey, Norman F. "August 1945: the B-29 Flight Logs," *Bulletin of Atom Scientists*, December 1982.

Stimson, Henry L. "The Decision to Use the Atomic Bomb," *Harper's*, February 1947.

INDEX

Alamogordo test. *See* Trinity
Allis-Chalmers Company, 43
Alvarez, Luis, 16–17
Anami, Korechika, 94
Atom splitting, discovery of, 21–23; *see also* Fission, atomic
Atom, structure of, 22–23
Atomic Energy Commission, 98
Atomic theory, history of, 21–26
Attlee, Clement, 84

Becquerel, Henri, 23
Belgian Congo, 32–33
Bock's Car, 14, 89
Bohr, Niels, 22, 24, 26, 33, 47
Bombing, conventional, 3
Bush, Vannevar, 36
Byrnes, James F., 55–56, 76–77, 79, 81, 101

Casualties: estimated, 11; at Hiroshima, 8–9; at Nagasaki, 15
Cavendish Laboratories, 24, 45
Chadwick, William, 57
Chain reaction, 25–26, 29–37; defined, 29–30; experiment at Columbia University, 30–31; first self-perpetuating, 33–37
Chiang Kai-shek, 60
Chicago Metallurgical Laboratory, 33–36, 49, 78–81; petition to warn Japan, 87
China, 60; Manchurian, 78–81
Chrysler Corporation, 43
Churchill, Winston, 53, 74, 78, *80,* 84–85
Cold War, 53–54, 98–99
Columbia University, 30–31, 33, 43, 52
Curie, Marie and Pierre, 23
Czechoslovakia, 31–32

Democritus, 21
Dooman, Eugene, 81–82

Einstein, Albert, 23–24, 32, 52, 98, 100
Electron discovered, 22
Emperor of Japan, 15, 78–82, 95
Eniwetok H-bomb test, 98
Enola Gay, 5, 6–8, 11, 16, 88; crew reports, 6–8

Fallout, 9, 66–67, 72
Fermi, Enrico, 28–29, 30–32, 63; and first chain reaction, 33–37, 42
Fission, atomic, 23–26; peacetime uses of, 26
Franck Report, 87
Frisch, Otto, 26, 29, 47
Fuchs, Klaus, 47, 50, 55, 84, 99

Gaseous diffusion, 31, 43
Germany: atomic research in, 24, 62; bombing of, 3; surrender of, 58–59
Göttingen, University of, 24, 45
Graham's law, 31
Great Britain, atomic research in, 36
Groves, Leslie R., 40, 64–65; justifies bomb, 85–86, 98; organizes Manhattan Project, 40–45; at Trinity test, 64–65, 67, 70

Hahn, Otto, 25–26, 29
Hahn-Strassman experiment, 25–26, 29
Hanford, Washington, plutonium plant, 43, 47–48
Harriman, Averell, 59
Hiroshima: bombing of, 6–14; today, 95, *97*
Hitler, Adolf, 21, 24, 26, 28, 32
Holloway, Marshall, 45–47
Houdaille-Hershey Corporation, 44
Hydrogen atoms, 22
Hydrogen bomb, 98–99

Implosion, 49–50
Invasion of Japan anticipated, 2, 53–54, 76–77

Japan: military code of, 94–95; postwar arms policy of, 95, 99; *see also* Emperor; Invasion; Peace Overtures; Surrender
Jewish scientists, importance of, 20–21, 24–26
Joliot-Curie, Irene and Frederic, 29., 30–31

Kamikaze planes, *75*, 76, 94

Laurence, William L.: describes Nagasaki bombing, 14–15; at Trinity test, 63–64, 70
Leahy, William, 86–87, 98

Lewis, Robert, 6–8
Los Alamos, 44–50

MacArthur, Douglas, *96*
Manchuria, Russian interest in, 78–81
Manhattan Project, 40–50, 52, 54; organized, 40–45; production problems, 48–49; scientists, 47; security, 47–48
Mass spectrometer, 31
Matsumoto, Shunichi, 82
Meitner, Lise, 25–26
Molotov, Vyacheslav, 79

Nagasaki bombing, 14–17, 88
Neutron identified, 22
Newton, Isaac, 21

Oak Ridge, Tennessee, plant, 31, 42–43, 47, 58
Office of Scientific Research and Development, 36
Okinawa, 76
Oppenheimer, J. Robert, 11, 17, 45, *46, 68;* endorses bomb, 87–88; opposes arms race, 98; at Trinity test, 62, 64, 67–69
Opposition to bomb, 86–87
Order to drop bomb, 85

Parsons, William S., 4, 47
Peace Memorial Park, Hiroshima, 95, *97*

Peace overtures from Japan, 78–81
Peierls, Rudolph, 47
Pile, first atomic, 33–36
Plutonium, 14, 36; plant, 37, 47–48
Plutonium bomb, 47–50, 59; at Nagasaki, 14–17; tested, *see* Trinity
Pontecorvo, Bruno, 47
Potsdam Conference, 59–60; and bomb test, 67, 70, 72, 77–78
Potsdam Declaration, 14, 81–83, 89

Radiation effects, 8, 65
Radioactivity discovered, 23
Research, atomic: before Manhattan Project, 28–37, 40–42; during Manhattan Project, 42–44, 49–50; prewar, 20–21, 23–26
Roentgen, Wilhelm, 23
Roosevelt, Franklin D., 32, 36, 40, 52–53, 55, 86; at Yalta, 53–56
Russia: arms race with, 98–99; enters war with Japan, 89; and Manchuria, 78–81; as possible ally against Japan, 53–54, 60, 67, 76–79, 83; U.S. relations with, 53–55, 59–60, 76–84
Rutherford, Ernest, 22

S-1 Committee, 36–37

Sachs, Alexander, 32, 52
Sata, Naotaki, 78–79
Seaborg, Glenn, 87
Secrecy, voluntary, 28, 31
Security, 4, 20, 36–37, 40, 43; at Los Alamos, 45, 47–48
Segré, Emilio, 47
Slotin, Louis, 45–47, 50
Spaatz, Carl, 85
Stalin, Joseph, 53, 74, 78–81, 83–84
Stimson, Henry L., 56–58, 72, 74–77, 86
Strassman, Fritz, 25–26
Styer, Wilhelm D., 40–41
Suicides, Japanese, 94–95
Surrender of Japan, 14–15, 89–92, 94–95, *96*; terms of, 58–60, 78–79
Survivor accounts, 8–9
Szilard, Leo, 28, 31–33, 47, 52, 87, 98–99

Teller, Edward, 24, 28, 32, 47, 52, 87–88, 98
Thomson, J. J., 22
Tibbets, Paul, *5,* 6–8
Tinian Island, 6
Togo, Shigenori, 78, 82
Trinity bomb test, 4, 14, 62–72; impact on Potsdam Conference, 59–60, 67, 70, 72, 77–78; press releases, 64, 70–72; radiation, 65–67, 72; schedule, 64, 67–68; site, 63–64; weather, 66–67
Truman, Harry S., 14, 17, 55, 72; briefed on bombs, 56–58; justifies bombings, 16–17, 85, 98; at Potsdam, 74–84

University of California at Berkeley, 36, 43
University of Chicago. *See* Chicago Metallurgical Laboratory
Uranium, 41, 47–49; atoms, 22–23; separating 235, 31, 42–43, 47, 49; sources, 32–33
Using the bomb: justified, 16–17, 84–86; opposed, 84–86

Van Kirk, Theodore, 6–8
Von Neumann, John, 47, 50

Warning Japan, 74–76, 87
Warren, Stafford, 66
Wheeler, John, 33
Wigner, John, 47

Yalta Conference, 53–56, 77–78
Yanaguchi, Tsutomu, 9

Zinn, Walter, 30

940.54
Cla

COMMUNITY UNIT SCH. DIST. #11
JR. H. S. LIBRARY
HOOPESTON, ILLINOIS

Chapter 2

12222

940.54
CLA
 Claypool, Jane
 Hiroshima and
 Nagasaki

12222

DATE DUE			